March '87   MARY   GRIFFITHS

TALES OF HORSEMEN

checked IM 11/93
ready to key
keyed IWN 11/93
checked PC/11/93

R. B. CUNNINGHAME GRAHAM

TALES
OF
HORSEMEN

edited and illustrated by
Alexander Maitland

CANONGATE
1981

First published in 1981 by
Canongate Publishing, 17 Jeffrey Street, Edinburgh

ISBN 0 903937 92 1 (hardback)

The publishers acknowledge
the financial assistance of the
Scottish Arts Council in the
publication of this volume

To the memory of
Violet Tschiffely and
Admiral Sir Angus Cunninghame Graham

Typeset in Scotland by Hewer Text Composition Services
Printed in Great Britain by
Lowe & Brydone Printers Ltd, Leeds, England

CONTENTS

Morcón   Cuchillar de Navajas   Alancasón

footing - Pico Cimo de Gredos   Feb/1980.

FOREWORD

When Robert Bontine Cunninghame Graham published *The Horses of the Conquest* in 1930 he dedicated the book to his favourite horse, the mustang he had rescued from a Glasgow horse-tram in the eighteen-eighties; the dedication reads:

> "To PAMPA – My black Argentine, who I rode for
> twenty years without a fall. May the earth lie on
> him as lightly as he once trod its face."

Pampa was the horse which shared the prime of my great-uncle Robert's life, the years of political and literary triumphs, the public acclaim, the disappointments, the striving, and the many notable friendships. This remarkable man would have lost much of his impact if he had walked to Westminster like other members of parliament; whereas Robert Cunninghame Graham, a direct descendant of Robert the Bruce, riding to the House of Commons on his shining black steed, was truly the chivalrous knight destined to right so many wrongs at a time of great change in our social history. It was on Pampa, too, that Robert rode beside his quiet, scholarly, adventurous wife, Gabrielle, as they toured their farms on the estate of Gartmore which circled the Lake of Menteith, with its three dark islands. These were the same lands which had belonged to the earls of Menteith, Robert's forebears, who had stood guard over the highland line for so many centuries, protecting the lowlanders from forays by the wild highlanders, even from Rob Roy himself.

Robert Cunninghame Graham had spent his boyhood at Gartmore in the eighteen-sixties, and it was here that he learned to love horses almost more than life itself. His family had all been natural horsemen, many of them passionate horsemen. It was his grandfather, Admiral Charles Elphinstone Fleeming, who had taken several couple of hounds from his own estate at Cumbernauld to the Calpé Hunt at Gibraltar, when serving there during the Peninsular War. At home, this same grandfather always hunted in Warwickshire, and attended every race meeting possible. It is even said that he rushed his little Spanish wife home to England for the Derby immediately after their grand wedding in the cathedral in Cadiz in 1815; and, on being unable to hire a suitable carriage at short notice, drove to the race-meeting in a hearse drawn by a team of black horses with nodding black plumes on their heads. His bride, Catalina, only fifteen years old, was in raptures of delight, imagining herself to be a young Infanta driving in state through the English countryside on that sunny June morning.

Robert's paternal grandmother was a member of another horse-loving family, the great Fitzwilliams from Yorkshire, and Robert was later to write with affectionate amusement about his eccentric English relations and their horsiness. In the sketch *Aunt Eleanor*, he gives a delightful picture of his Aunt Helen Speirs, his grandmother's sister, whose chief themes of conversation were horses and hunting, setting out her theories as to which rein should go under which finger, and how good hands consisted in the wrist. "It is all done with a turn of the wrist, my dear, and not by butchering", she would say to her favourite great-nephew, Robert, and he followed her advice with enthusiasm, feeling her theories to be sound and wise, and grateful for this competent aunt who taught him so much.

Horses were an integral part of Robert's life at Gartmore, so his riding was taken for granted and seldom mentioned; but not long ago, in a bundle of boyhood letters from Robert and his younger brother, Charlie, to their mother, I found a blotchy missive written at Moffat in 1863 by Charlie who was spending a holiday with an aunt and uncle, Robert being at prep school in Warwickshire by then.

"My dear Mama," he wrote, "I hope you are quite well. I like Moffat very much. Uncle Tom has given me a fishing rod and I have fished twice in the Annan but caught nothing. We drove to Lockwood and I looked into the dungeon, there was a wood of fine old oaks round the ruins. I wrote to Robert and told him that his poney [sic] had a foal. When I go to Gartmore is my pony to go with me? – As I cannot ride Robert's. Give my love to Papa. I am your affectionate son, C.E.F.C. Graham."

In this little letter comes the first inkling that his brother Robert, older by two years, is already an accomplished horseman, riding a lively mare which Charlie finds unmanageable.

But it was not until Robert went to work on the Ogilvy's estancia in Entre Rios, Argentina, seven years later, that his love of horses seems to have become his *raison d'être*. Robert's own letters to his mother, in his impossibly illegible handwriting (later to be a nightmare to all printers' compositors) talk of nothing but horses: his first letter from Buenos Aires in 1870 comments with delight that horses are commoner than dogs in this city of "fine airs": "They stand at every house with their feet hobbled while their owners talk or drink. Now and then they get bored and hop off like rocking horses, to congregate in knots, where, with their reins tied to their saddles, drawing their heads into their chests, they stand and fabulate."

On the steamer to Guleguaychú Robert met his first group of gauchos, and listened fascinated as they talked endlessly about horses, and scratched brands on the deck with their *facones* (long gaucho knives) to the annoyance of the captain. Robert, already bilingual in Spanish, soon began to understand the gauchos' strange dialect, and heard them talking of the characteristics of different coloured horses: how greys will not stand the sun, how the roan is slow, and the horse with a white fore and white hind foot is sure to be fast, how a dun horse will never be any good unless he has a dark tail and mane and red eyes, and how the horse that is chestnut with a white mane and tail is only good for prostitutes.

For the next eight years Robert was to become inseparable from horses; he spent all day in the saddle roaming the pampas while herding cattle or lassoing wild horses in the company of his friends the gauchos.

It was in Paraguay that he bought the first horse he was to grow deeply fond of. There were three special horses in Robert's life,

Bunny (or el Blanco), Pampa, and Chajá. Bunny was the horse of his adventurous youth, Pampa the horse of his manhood, and Chajá the gentle horse of his old age. Bunny, a grey, took him on an expedition which lasted four months as he rode for six hundred miles through the jungles and swamps of Paraguay, prospecting for yerbales, areas in which to grow yerba maté for making green tea, after the economy of Paraguay had plunged to rock bottom following the terrible war of the Triple Alliance.

Sadly, Robert's only business venture fell through from lack of investment, and he had to leave both Paraguay and his beloved old grey horse, to return to Gartmore. But Bunny had taught Robert that a horse could be the best companion of all. He had the special qualities that made him a good 'journey horse', the most useful of all being his lazy nature. A horse that is not too anxious to exert itself will always have the greatest endurance, and a keener horse than Bunny would have exhausted itself far too quickly on the long and arduous journeys through swamp and jungle as Robert explored the Alto Parana between July and November of 1872. Bunny returned to Asuncion in fine condition and Robert was able to write to his mother that the horse was now the proud possessor of his first set of shoes: "at first he tried to rub them off on posts and things, but now he is reconciled to them and rather proud of them!"

Robert and Bunny soon became well known to the Brazilian troops who guarded the Paraguayan government offices in Asuncion after the war, and were greeted cheerfully by the black Brazilian soldiers as they rode past. On one occasion Robert had to leave Bunny in the middle of a narrow street while he made a purchase in a shop, and emerging, was amused to see a platoon of black soldiers trying to decide how to pass this obstacle with military dignity. After a long consultation with their sergeant, they decided to march past on either side of the horse, leaving him in the middle of the street, and each in turn patting him and saying "What a good horse you are, Bunny!" as they passed. Robert was convulsed with mirth, and amazed that it had not occurred to them to lead Bunny to one side so that the two columns of soldiers could pass by more easily. Bunny got rather tired of being admired in this way and grabbed the last soldier's cap off his head as he marched past "chewing it fearfully before I could rescue it."

To leave a country of which the horse was so vital a part was a heartbreak to Robert. He managed to return to Argentina in 1876 for another spell of two years, in partnership with a retired naval officer, running an estancia in Bahia Blanca, and greatly assisted by an ex-revolutionary foreman who branded every horse in sight, just like Colonel Maverick in Texas. But then Robert's father became seriously ill, and he had to return to the family estates in Scotland. Two years later he was married to Gabrielle, and the couple spent a two-year honeymoon in Texas and Mexico, once more surrounded by horses, hopefully looking for ranch-land to buy. But this proved to be a wild goose chase, so back they came to Scotland to settle at Gartmore, and to content themselves with riding over the hills, or down to the Lake of Menteith through the rushy parks. It was then that Pampa came into their lives, providing Robert with a welcome link with Argentina. (The brand on his flank was none other than the brand used by one of the estancieros he had known, Eduardo Casey.) Gabrielle acquired a small Icelandic pony which was called Talla after the island on which the old Graham castle had stood for so many years in the sanctuary of the lake. Gabrielle did not survive her pony long, and both were dead by 1906, but Pampa continued to carry his master proudly for many more years, until he went to spend his retirement on a farm in Surrey, where he finally died in 1911.

The last of the three horses, Chajá, was a retired polo pony from Argentina, destined to carry Don Roberto (now an ageing horseman, but still capable of jumping on to his steed, bending low to pick a glove from the ground as he galloped past) for the last two decades of his life. Chajá was to outlive his master by five years, and to carry me as a child of ten over the tidal sands downstream from Dumbarton Rock at Ardoch, where we went to live on my great-uncle's death in 1936.

And so I was privileged to ride one of the trio of great horses who had carried Don Roberto so proudly, and as I cantered over the hard sand I could feel the gentle mouth and the responsive intuition of the horse. It was almost as though my great-uncle was teaching me to ride himself.

I like to think that it was Don Roberto's love of horses that introduced us to the gentle side of his nature. Reading the stories that form this book, it is easy to see this aspect of the man who cared so passionately for the well-being of the horses who served him faithfully and well. They were his loyal and devoted friends, and he treated them accordingly. But he knew that they were as different as they could be from each other. They had their own unique characters, their own ways of being funny, of being affectionate, and of being tiresome. He enjoyed their idiosyncrasies and he felt they gave him more reliable friendship than the human race. Men were fickle and self-seeking, horses were faithful and selfless.

Robert Cunninghame Graham hardly ever hunted to hounds, but we know that he enjoyed attending race meetings. It is certain, however, that he enjoyed the gauchos' races in Argentina and Paraguay a great deal more than social events such as Ascot and the Derby, and perhaps it was in memory of those exciting races in Entre Rios that he always wore his gaucho knife under his morning coat at Ascot – as was once revealed to a friend who caught a glimpse of the weapon when Don Roberto bent down to pick up a dropped race card. Robert Cunninghame Graham was a man for all seasons and a man for all people, but his true self is revealed in a letter to his mother written in Paraguay in 1872 when he was twenty years old.

"I care very little about the Menteith peerage, as long as no-one else gets it. I would have to sit at rich men's feasts in a sort of second-hand way. As to taking part in that sort of entertainment, I would rather share a handful of maize with 'el Blanco' out on the plains."

On Don Roberto's memorial there is a plaque depicting the head of his black Argentine, Pampa. Beneath it the inscription reads:

"Famous Author, Traveller, and Horseman. Patriotic Scot and Citizen of the World. He was a Master of Life, a King among Men."

To Robert Bontine Cunninghame Graham there was only one quality he would have recognised out of this impressive list, and I can imagine him smiling with amusement as he dismissed the rest, smoothing back his white hair with that familiar gesture and saying, "A *horseman*, yes . . . for what, indeed, would be the point of living in a world without horses?"

Jean Polwarth
Harden
Hawick

INTRODUCTION

I

Although most people who are seriously interested in horses and almost everyone who is interested in South America will have heard of Cunninghame Graham, it is undeniable that to some he may be less well known, and to others even, not at all. With the latter in mind, therefore, a few brief notes about his life may be useful. Robert Bontine Cunninghame Graham was born in London on 24 May 1852, into an aristocratic Scottish landowning family with maternal Spanish connections. He lived vigorously, without compromise, and died full of dignity and years, in Buenos Aires, on 20 March 1936. By returning to Argentine at the close of a varied and eventful life, it may be assumed that Cunninghame Graham was deliberately renewing, for the last time, acquaintance with his spiritual home; taking one last, long look at the windswept plains of his youth. "Pája y cielo", he used to call them; "all grass and sky, and sky and grass, and still more sky and grass."

When he came first to the Argentine in 1870 after a conventional upbringing in search of adventure, dreaming of fortunes to be made, the character of the pampas had altered little during the thirty or so years since Rosas' Indian reprisals, or the idyllic childhood of W. H. Hudson. Indians still occasionally raided outlying settlements, burned houses, murdered the menfolk, drove off horses and cattle and disembowelled or appropriated the women. The isolated *pulperias*, or wayside inns, harboured drunken gauchos and bandits of the traditional, cold-blooded kind, who would cut a man's throat for a look, or the few *centavos* in his pocket. In the course of eight years spent largely, though by no means continuously, in Argentina, Uruguay, Paraguay and Brazil, Cunninghame Graham committed these wild people and events to memory and wrote about them in spontaneous, lively letters which he sent spasmodically to his mother. While first ranching with the Ogilvy's in the province of Entre Rios, afterwards driving wild horses north with his partner, Lieutenant Mansel, for sale to the Brazilian army, Cunninghame Graham had many narrow escapes. On one occasion, we are told, having been pursued and captured by Indians, he managed to get away only after stabbing his incautious guard to death.

From 1879 until 1881, Cunninghame Graham travelled extensively throughout Texas and Mexico with his nineteen year old bride, Gabrielle. During these journeys, he dabbled in ranching, shipping, property and the cotton trade, accompanied buffalo hunting parties over the prairies, and in Mexico taught fencing under the pseudonym, "Professor Bontini". While he was thus employed, Gabrielle kept herself busy by giving lessons in French conversation and the guitar; and by sketching the ruined Jesuit missions.

In 1883, Cunninghame Graham's father died after many years of chronic illness, leaving him at the age of thirty-two, the large, somewhat run down family estate, Gartmore, in Perthshire, close to the Lake of Menteith. The following years were devoted to improving the property, but the young couple's efforts met with little success. Gartmore continued to decline until, in 1900, it eventually had to be sold. Not content with merely farming, between 1886 and 1892, Cunninghame Graham represented the mining constituency of North-west Lanark as a Gladstonian Liberal. He fought untiringly in and out of Parliament to improve the living and working conditions of coalminers and factory workers, whom he regarded as victims of an unfair class-system, of exploitation and of the consequent, unequal distribution of wealth. The fact of his own aristocratic background in no way deterred him; nor indeed dampened the affection of his working-class constituents.

In January 1888, Cunninghame Graham was sent to prison for six weeks for his part in the Trafalgar Square riots of the previous November. He had led a rush against the police cordon surrounding the Square, gathered there, it now transpires, quite illegally – to prevent speeches of protest being made by leaders of a march in support of Irish patriots gaoled in their fight for Home Rule.

Throughout the twenty-eight years of their marriage, Cunninghame Graham and his wife travelled regularly every year in France, Spain, Italy or North Africa; occasionally together, more often separately. Gabrielle followed miles of lonely mountain tracks in the footsteps of the great Spanish saint, Teresa of Avila, whose biography she wrote. Graham roamed the stony wildernesses of Morocco, once during 1897 in disguise; besides which he made journeys to Andorra and the Rhône delta. Once he searched fruitlessly for a Lusitanian gold-mine, about which Gabrielle had read in Pliny in the library at Gartmore, and visited the beautiful Spanish glens of the Batuecas, discovered by Gabrielle in the course of her wanderings. This peripatetic mode of life continued until the late summer of 1906, when Gabrielle, whose health had been deteriorating over a long period, died of tuberculosis at Hendaye, near Biarritz.

Between 1895 and 1936, Cunninghame Graham published over thirty books, including collections of essays and stories numbering about two hundred. Besides these, he wrote newspaper articles, reviews and prefaces on a wide variety of topics from politics to pioneering, from the lamentable maltreatment of British labour to the abuse of horses in the Spanish bull-rings. His last years were lonely, in spite of an attentive residue of friends, old and new, that included Edward Garnett, Oscar Wilde, Wilfred Scawen Blunt, W. H. Hudson, Joseph Conrad and George Bernard Shaw.

Garnett discovered many writers at the end of the nineteenth century and directed Cunninghame Graham's energies into new channels when he told him, "The man of action must now become the artist," and set him on the path to literary fame. Cunninghame Graham was always grateful for his friend's gentle encouragement and his appreciation of the unique style of literary impressionism which had not began to emerge until Graham's early forties. Wilde, Graham liked always, but thought him a "kind hearted & generous fool". Blunt, who like Graham, "touched like at a hundred different points", entertained him in the strange, Middle-Eastern twilight of his Sussex home, Newbuildings Place and was, like Graham, wealthy; besides, a squire and a gentleman. Blunt had also served a prison sentence for his part in the fight for Irish Home Rule, had travelled with desert tribesmen in Arabia and, with his wife, Lady Anne, founded the famous Crabbet Arab horse stud. Conrad's childhood had been very similar to Cunninghame Graham's, and they were originally drawn together because of these similarities – fatherless from an early age, the sons of aristocrats, seeking their respective fortunes by land and sea, far from their native countries. Only in their attitudes to politics were they total opposites, and even this type of disagreement stimulated their friendship still further. Cunninghame Graham's encouragement seemed to come as an essential part of Conrad's ability to write, and Graham was later to tell his friends that he had often assisted at the "Caesarian Operation", which was the only way Conrad could deliver a masterpiece.

Shaw used Cunninghame Graham's larger-than-life, almost fictional personality as the basis for characters in three of his plays, *The Devil's Disciple*, *Heartbreak House* and *Arms and the Man*. A fourth play, *Captain Brassbound's Conversion*, was based directly upon Graham's exploits in Morocco, in particular *Mogreb-el-Acksa*, his account of an abortive attempt to reach the forbidden city of Tarudant, in the Sus. Hudson, large-boned, gaunt, poor in middle life, was no less intimate than the rest and he and Graham would talk enthusiastically for hours about South America and the old life on the pampas. In ways, Graham reflected aspects of them all, just as they each found in him a particular shade of delight or inspiration.

Graham supplemented Gabrielle's loss to an extent by his friend-ship with a rich, cultivated widow, "Toppie" Dummett, with whom he travelled frequently abroad. In 1932, his meeting with Aimé Felix Tschiffely, thirty-seven year old hero of a ten thousand mile horse-back ride from Buenos Aires to Washington, filled a gap caused by Hudson's death ten years before. Like Hudson, Tschiffely knew South America, spoke Spanish, loved horses and regarded Cunninghame Graham with a kind of awe; something the older man must have found appealing, being also somewhat vain.

Shortly before his death, Cunninghame Graham made a pilgrimage to Hudson's birthplace in Argentina, "The House of the Twenty-five Ombus", and breathed again, for the last time, the pure, sweet pampas' air. In this spacious country, scattered with ostriches and shy guanacos, so perfectly attuned to travel with horses, Graham had found unique freedom, identity and a rich aboriginal happiness. There is much of these elements in the stories which follow.

He was never a man to be shackled to a profession, certainly none that entailed the smallest degree of subservience to another individual. It has been suggested, nevertheless, that Graham was at least sub-servient to the craft of letters. Yet his writing, driven in a rush of imagery and ideas, would be dashed out, mostly by lamplight, in the jagged, barely decipherable scrawl that was the printer's nightmare; and which, completed, spelled the temporary end to concern for the particular piece of work. In spite of chiding by friends such as Conrad, proofs were merely glanced at; corrections scribbled hit-and-miss, or left to his mother who did her best to tidy them. It was all part of Cunninghame Graham's volatile character which dispersed its energies like solar bursts, seemingly at random, with little coherent or immediately identifiable purpose.

Cunninghame Graham, as we might say in the present context, took life as far as possible at the gallop, heedless of obstacles, man-fully bearing the crashes when they came. As a writer, politician, social-reformer, traveller, horseman and adventurer, he was un-questionably one of the most extraordinary – though curiously unremarked – figures of his day, even if, by inclination, he had been born four hundred years too late, or, as a social thinker, half a century ahead of his time. A kind of historical nomad, Cunninghame Graham trod an uneasy tightrope and it is the resulting tension that gives his life and writings such wild savour and esoteric glamour, especially attractive at a period in which individualism is looked upon with suspicion as an outmoded, even misanthropic, indulgence.

II

The first of Cunninghame Graham's biographers, Herbert Faulkner West, has given valuable information about Graham's skills and en-durance as a horseman. He rode, according to West (and by his own admission), like a gaucho, mounting and re-mounting at intervals during a long journey to rest his horse; unlike his Arab acquaintances in Morocco who believed that such procedures fatigue the animal more than the road. "In his youth", West tells us, "Cunninghame Graham sometimes rode from 90 to 103 miles in 24 hours." West owed these statistics to conversations with Graham during the preparation of *A Modern Conquistador*, and to references in his sketches.

Mounted, Graham sat, not in the English fashion, but like a *vacquero*, or an American cowboy, "that is, with hand held high, and palate bit, and on a saddle differing scarcely at all from those used by the conquerors." Thus Tschiffely described his technique, still flawless at more than eighty years of age. Tschiffely had reached Ardoch, Dunbartonshire, where the Cunninghame Grahams had moved after Gartmore, after a forty-three day ride from Wiltshire. In *Bridle Paths*, he wrote: ". . . as soon as I had dismounted (Cunninghame Graham) took my place in the saddle, mounting . . . with the ease and agility of a *gaucho*. Sitting erect, and skilfully guiding the mare with the lightest of touches on the neck and mouth, he made her go up and down a few times, twisting and turning her round as if his thoughts were transmitted to the animal's brain through the bridles which hung half slack, resting on the first finger of the rider's left hand. As I watched man and beast go through a few evolutions, I had visions of a cavalier preparing to go into an arena for a joust."

West included in his book a photograph of Cunninghame Graham, dated November 1931, on his last horse, El Chajá, in the exact posture so meticulously recorded by Tschiffely.

For all that he was so experienced, like everyone who rides hard and continually, in all conditions, Cunninghame Graham now and then came a cropper. In 1929, aged seventy-six, writing to West from Tenerife, Graham observed: "An incident with the lazo in youth, stirred up last spring in Venezuela *helping to saddle a wild mule*, has made my writing almost unintelligible." (The italics are part of the quotation.) Or, again, in a letter dated June 1931, Graham asked West: "Did I tell you of my turn with the Argentine buckjumper? I thought I had finished "with all that", but no. I sat seven, counting them as I used to in the old days and preparing to "fan" with my hat. Then my head went, and I should have gone, but the mare saw to that, for crouching low, she put my left foot on the ground, and I turned right over on my back not hurt, or even shaken, and when I got on her again, she went off like an old cow, neither frightened or excited . . . sure sign of a bad one."

Cunninghame Graham dedicated one of his last books, *The Horses of the Conquest*, to Pampa, "the black Argentine" with whom he will always be associated. An unashamed, eccentric gesture, it was saved from an excess of sentiment by the fine, terse writing that followed, an extract from which is reprinted here.

Much as he would later exalt them, Cunninghame Graham, being also a little practical, had acknowledged from his earliest years the horse's Chekovian role of compromising servitude. *The Horses of the Conquest* derived from a story, "The Horses of the Pampas" and from the author's days and nights spent herding half-broken mustangs or chasing wild cattle; watching the mottled herd as they jostled forward on the trail, raising dust or sleek and ragged-maned in the drenching rain. He overlooked them from the saddle, seeing them whipped and cursed through broad, fast-flowing rivers; swimming strongly, all submerged except for their heads, blue-eyed with fear; now and then, sinking without trace. The gauchos accepted such accidents philosophically, disinterested, evasive, concerned with their own survival and the survival of the remainder of the *tropilla*. The horses' colours, unimaginably various, gave Graham in old age the opportunity to show off his quite exceptional powers of recall by reciting them unalphabetically, as they came to mind; a kaleidoscopic flood, disordered, each of its separate elements, like the animal, struggling for position; a *tour de force* and a testament to Graham's wide understanding, acute observation, insatiable thirst for knowledge and tireless anxiety to memorise and retain those teeming shades of long ago. In all his writing there may be found references to horses; for example, the biography, *Jose Antonio Páez*, in which Páez remarks that white horses are the best swimmers. Graham agrees, recalling as evidence in one of his inevitable footnotes, one such animal he himself had owned and ridden in Paraguay that swam high in the water, carrying "his head erect, like a water snake."

In the 1870s, when the pampas were still full of danger, a horse that swam well, had strong wind and could cover long distances, finding speed when necessary, without much need of rest, or grass, or water, was worth its weight in gold. For upon his horse, not infrequently, the rider's life depended. Such a beast, however ugly, was prized far above the gentler, elegant sort, well-mannered but easily blown, from which a man might be dragged by a shrieking war-party, to be held prisoner at some distant camp, the soles of his feet having been flayed to prevent escape. The prospect of rescue was slender; the only certain release, a slowly articulated, agonising death by torture. Between this terrible fate and freedom stood a good horse, strong and capable of carrying a man ninety miles a day without complaint. (A fact against which Cunninghame Graham's long-distance rides should be assessed.) An experienced, intelligent horse would avoid burrows and sun-cracks so that, even at night, as Hudson has recorded, it would be possible for the rider to lie flat along its back, guiding the animal gently with his feet, and watch the stars drift slowly overhead.

Cunninghame Graham has admitted wryly that, in common with all horsemen, and like theologians, he was intolerant and biased in favour of what he knew. "Believe my faith," he wrote, "and ride my horse after my fashion, for no non-conformist, Cossack, Anglican, Gaucho, Roman Catholic or Mexican can see the least redeeming point in his fellow's creed, his saddle, horse, ox, ass, or any other thing belonging to him." Thus, when in London, Graham cantered in the Row in the manner that best pleased him and, in his opinion, best suited his horse. Shunning contemptuously the fashion for docked tails, he allowed Pampa's to sweep the ground, falling loose, like the tail of any wild horse.

Cunninghame Graham's knowledge of horses, like his experience, is beyond question. These, gained at first hand on the pampas, besides Mexico, Texas, Spain and Morocco, illuminate his work, as they infused his being; becoming, as it were, his brand. Without such a wealth of experience he would never have written – indeed never could have written – of horses and horsemen as he did. It is therefore neither accidental nor surprising that when his friend, Sir John Lavery, set about his portrait, he did not paint Cunninghame Graham either addressing a political rally or surveying his estates, or seated, writing, in his study. Instead, Lavery painted him, wearing a sombrero, aloof and splendid, moving easily astride Pampa across the southern plains, his eyes fixed on the receding, far horizon.

III

The following selection of stories and essays opens with a long extract from a full-length self explanatory work, *The Horses of the*

Conquest, first published in 1930, which sets the scene and provides both atmosphere and historical perspective. Here, as elsewhere, Cunninghame Graham reveals his sharp eye for detail, be it of dress, or saddlery, or speech or gait. He evokes the spirit of the Conquistadores, seated, like gauchos, at their lonely fires, writing their daily adventures in "vigorous Castilian". Graham vividly conveys the moods of changing weather, spirits up the wind, unleashes the tropical torrent and bares the cruel sun. We are made to realise that this same sun shone on Conquistador, Indian and gaucho alike, as Graham chisels in stark relief, in other tales, feature upon feature of the harsh, gaucho existence, its sudden, almost shocking, pleasures and slants of unexpected beauty.

Since camp-fire talk on the plains, all through the Americas must necessarily range over horses, cattle, ostrich-hunting and so forth, Cunninghame Graham has given in an early volume, *The Ipané*, two consecutive essays, *The Lazo* and *The Bolas*, in which we learn something of the origin and the practice of each. In *El Rodeo*, published in 1913, he includes vibrant snapshots, in a series of which a gaucho lazoes a bullock, "the thin hide-plaited rope . . shining and glistening in the sun . . . winding like a snake (as it) hurtled through the air." Catching a wild bullock and killing with the *façon*, the long-bladed gaucho knife, could be dangerous work that often ended with a *peon* impaled on the lunging horns.

Many gifted men, including the writers, José Hernández and Ricardo Güiraldes, had ridden there and seen these and other such thrilling sights but, until Cunninghame Graham (and, as Cunninghame Graham would have insisted, Darwin, W. H. Hudson, and the railway engineer, Crawford) had had the urge or the ability to write about them in English; it fell to Cunninghame Graham to give the landscape and its distinctive races of men and animals a wider immortality, preserving them in their time, like the tapestries of a vanished world. W. H. Hudson, entombed in Bayswater, relived the pampas of his youth in beautiful tales of birds and flowers and children, the latter wild and innocent like the animals. Although, like Cunninghame Graham, a gaucho and a prose-poet, Hudson's early work, for example *Idle Days in Patagonia*, differs from Graham's by virtue of its almost exclusive concern for the birdlife, flowers and country. It might be argued that such writing also lacks the vitality which human contact brings to the narratives of Cunninghame Graham.

"Singularissimo escritor inglés," Hudson called his friend; a generous, yet plainly honest, appraisal of Cunninghame Graham's unique recordings of the pampas' scene. Cunninghame Graham's portraits are, indeed, no less perceptively drawn than his landscapes. Frequently they are exotic, as in *The Grave of the Horseman*, where he pictures a sheikh, Si Omar, returning in the wake of his followers after a raid. The sheikh proceeds on his way, tense, constantly aware of the fine balance between sovereignty and death, controlling his men by fear, never certain of their loyalty. Inadvertently, still it seems in a manner appropriate to the sheikh's uneasy rule, his white horse, stumbling, brings down Si Omar and his reign in the same awkward movement. A Berber, one of his clan, rides up and shoots him where he lies, remarking, "God wishes it; Si Omar's day is done." Here are two aspects of Cunninghame Graham's writing: man, the victim of chance, yet quick to use chance to further his own ends.

In the weird, twilight world of *Snaekoll's Saga*, unlike any other of Cunninghame Graham's stories having been set in Iceland (a country he had once visited with his brother Charles in the 1870s), the horse is again cast in a sinister role. Snaekoll, a misshapen, evil-tempered brute, is portrayed in some depth and given as much a character as his young master, Thorgrimur Hjaltalin. Hjaltalin is a temperamental dreamer who determines to risk his life and his horse in an attempt to cross the Vatna Jokull, a huge icefield never before traversed in his generation. The journey may be seen as an act of supreme selfishness, just as it seems to Hjaltalin's wife unreasonable and pointless. Unless, she ponders, half-admiring, "Thorgrimur in reading Sagas had come upon the whereabouts of some great treasure buried in times gone by." However, greed is not Hjaltalin's driving force.

The grotesque little pony, Snaekoll, is a caricature of survival: unromantic, mindlessly practical, tenuous to life. Hjaltalin symbolises the magnificence of failure, the ultimate significance of the unrealised ideal. Regarded coldly and dispassionately, many of Graham's own best efforts ended, like Hjaltalin's, in failure. All his business ventures; all his and Gabrielle's strivings to make Gartmore a going concern; his sojourn in the mess of party politics; his losing battle against the blight of progress and the spreading stain of civilisation that would blot out the pampas' life for ever. Yet, in common with the Icelander, these failures have in them a quality that ordinary achievement lacks.

Had Cunninghame Graham, for instance, perished in the North African foothills, never having written *Mogreb-el-Acksa*, his journey to Tarudant might have brought him nearer to greatness in men's eyes. An acknowledged champion of failure, Graham nevertheless showed himself quick to appreciate genuine success, as his narrative of *Tschiffely's Ride* exemplifies. Written in 1932, from newspaper reports, the story tells of the epic journey from South into North America made by a former Swiss schoolmaster together with Mancha and Gato, two middle-aged *criollo* ponies. When Tschiffely arrived in London, having failed inexplicably to sell his book, Cunninghame Graham gave him lunch, read the manuscript and, within a few days, had successfully placed what was destined to become a best-seller with his publishers, William Heinemann.

Contrary to their effect on his imagination, Tschiffely's impress upon the countries through which he passed had been slight, an important feature which distinguishes the traveller from the explorer, or the explorer's jackal, the colonist. Cunninghame Graham could only approve. Men's passage through the wild Arcadias, he would tolerate, even admire. What stuck in his gullet was the litter of immigrant trade and the imposition of immigrant culture, such as he reviles in *Feast Day in Santa Maria Mayor*: "cheap European trifles . . . little looking-glasses in pewter frames . . . gaudy pictures representing saints."

Vilifying progress and its concomitant evils, viewing with sadness and futile rage the passing of life as he had known it on the South American plains, Mexico and North Africa, Cunninghame Graham was perhaps unconsciously mourning his own lost years, knowing that youth had slipped irretrievably away. By recalling the vanished pampas' modes, he may have been summoning his young manhood for a time, wearing it like a tightly-fitting garment, painfully writing it out of his system in the half-darkness of the study at Ardoch. Hernández's gaucho classic, *Martín Fierro*, had first appeared when Graham was twenty, ranching and travelling on the pampas. In those days, not so far removed from the equestrian teachings of *Aunt Eleanor* (in real life, his grandmother's sister, Helen Speirs), he had worn the traditional gaucho costume: wide, baggy trousers (*bombachas*), short boots, iron spurs with immense, starred rowels, a beret or a sombrero, coloured sash, poncho and neckerchief. For protection, he carried pistols and a *façon*. He rode horses of every shape and size, all colours, some of them slothful, others, like *The Stationmaster's Horse*, a little hard to mount. Cunninghame Graham worshipped the life and its semi-theatrical glamour, which was in many respects what the Roman Catholic creed is to Christianity: mysterious, full of strange ceremony, greatly dependant upon the suspension of cold reason; a hot-blooded, uncompromising affair employing no half-measures. So too the country, where no middle plane apparently existed; nothing to mediate between the over-whelming vastness and the microcosm of tiny flowers, insects, stones and vegetation.

In the pampas' life, full of space and horses, sentiment also had its place in the stories told round lonely fires by dark-skinned guttural-spoken men, huddled in blankets, sucking hot maté noisily through silver straws. There, beside them, or in the saddle, Cunninghame Graham had found himself, and the necessary alternative culture so often sought by Europeans. It came to him gradually over the years, colourful, potent and enduring; a love of existence for its own sake, as much as of the horses and the gauchos who rode them, glued to their backs, like centaurs.

That his work never received its due place in his lifetime is nothing new and even apt. Like the acquisition of wisdom, Cunninghame Graham's literary reputation and the recognition of his greater signifi-cance has been slow to build. The stories which follow show many facets of his nature; there is in them a little of everything. But a part of the man, they are yet much more than the man. They give no comprehensive picture of his life, yet they tell, better than any biography, the strength of his feelings, the shrewdness of his intel-lect, his passions, shortcomings, knowledge of the world and his true place in it. These things alone may be gleaned from a man's work (Cunninghame Graham is no exception) besides which, even the most exhaustively documented Life is about as revealing of his soul as the buttons on his coat.

Alexander Maitland,
Edinburgh

THE HORSES OF THE CONQUEST (II)

If Cortés was the first of the Spanish writers on the New World to insert, even in the reports he sent the Emperor, references and anecdotes of the horses who did so much to make the Conquest possible, it was to Bernal Diaz del Castillo that we owe the names, the qualities and colours of many of the horses that, as he says, "accompanied us to this Conquest."

Cortés wrote as a captain occupied with the events of the great adventure in which he was engaged. Although himself a horseman, writing to Charles the Prince of Light Horsemen, as his soldiers called him, when he mentions anything that happened to his horses he writes of horses, and not as Bernal Diaz writes, as if they had been voluntary companions and sharers of the perils and the hardships of the campaign. Cortés of course was ignorant of the fate that befell his black horse (el Morzillo) or certainly he would have compared him to the horse that Lucius Verres deified, and fed upon the incongruous diet of almonds and raisins, perhaps to fit him for the skies.

How he behaved has not been preserved; but he remained but a short time amongst the Olympians, not long enough to have acquired the semi-cynical, non-committal attitude of his state, for he was but a parvenu in Olympus, compared to the Morcillo of Cortés.

As the chief object of Bernal Diaz was to preserve the names, the qualities and the exploits of his fellow-soldiers from the oblivion into which mere writers of the study, such as Gómara, had consigned them, so did he the like, for those to whom "after God we owed the Conquest."

Warworn, and at the age of eighty-four, not over-blessed in this world's goods, the intrepid veteran embarked upon the stormy sea of letters, and produced a masterpiece. Though naturally Bernal Diaz rises to greater heights in speaking of his companions, it is in writing of the horses that his full kindliness and simplicity appears. Though fifty years or more had passed, he hardly ever mentions one of them, without referring to its colour or its qualities. One feels that he had ridden, fed and'led to water almost all of them. On many a scorching day he must have nodded on their backs; through the night watches he must have fought with sleep, and those who like him have sat stiff, sore, and tired, waiting for dawn, as a man waits for a mistress who has delayed, to paint her face or take one last peep in the looking-glass, are in communion with him.

From the beginning of his history Bernal Diaz begins to talk about the horses. Firstly, of the difficulty of procuring any, for they were scarce and dear in Cuba, in which island Cortés was fitting out his fleet for Mexico. "When all was ready," he says, "we embarked the horses and set up mangers in the ships for them to eat from." Their food was maize and hay. "I wish to put down," he says, "from memory, all the horses and the mares that we embarked. Captain Cortés, a black bay which died in San Juan de Ulua." As San Juan de Ulua is the first port they touched at, Captain Cortés got but little benefit by his black bay.

"Pedro de Alvarado and Hernando Lopez de Avila, a bright bay mare. She turned out very good, both for tilting and to race, when we got to New Spain (Mexico). Pedro de Alvarado either bought the other share of her (from Lopez de Avila), or else took it by force. Alonzo Hernandez, a grey mare. She was fast, and Cortés bought her (for Puertocarrero) for a gold shoulder knot. Juan Velazquez de Léon, another grey mare, and she was very strong. We called her Bobtail. She too was fast, and had a splendid mouth. Christobel de Oli, a dark bay, a very good horse. Francisco de Montejo and Alonso de Avila, a dark chestnut horse; he was no good for war." Bernal Diaz for a wonder does not say what was the matter with the dark chestnut. It may have been (as he was a chestnut) that like the horse Pascasas that Cyrus rode on the day of his defeat, he was hot and impossible to hold.

It is hard upon a horse to have his shortcomings preserved in history and brought up against him, after a lapse of centuries. However Bernal Diaz was as Draconian both in his praise and blame to horses as to men. "Another man who came with us we called Beberreo, for he was a mighty drinker," may be put against the chestnut that was not fit for war.

"Francisco de Morla had a dark bay, very fast and well bitted. Juan de Escalante a light bay with three white feet. He was no good. Diego de Ordas a grey mare. She was barren and a pacer, but not fast. Gonzalo Dominguez (a first-rate rider) a very good and fast dark brown horse.

"Pedro Gonzalez de Truxillo, a good bay horse, that turned out very fast. Vaena, from La Trinidad, a piebald horse, inclining to black in the markings, with white forefeet; he turned out worthless. Moron of Vaimo, a piebald with white feet and a very good mouth.

"Lares, the fine horseman, a good horse, bay in colour, but rather light, a good galloper, Ortiz the musician and one Bartolomé Garcia, who had gold mines, a good black horse, that was called the Drover. He was one of the good horses that we took aboard the fleet. Juan Sedeño from the Habana, a brown mare, and this mare had a foal on board the ship. This Juan Sedeño was the richest soldier in the fleet, for he had a vessel of his own and the mare, together with a negro and much cassava bread and bacon.

"In those days there was no horses to be got or negroes either, except at a great price, and that was why we embarked no more horses for there were hardly any to be had."

Thus after fifty years, each horse and mare stepped into history. This equine roll-call is at the same time a priceless human document, for it throws a light that Bernal Diaz and he alone has turned upon the fitting out of an expedition from the Antillas to the mainland, in those conquering days. It also lets us see, incidentally, into Bernal Diaz's own mentality, and shows him, the careful, kindly old Castilian that he was, sparing of words, but using them as skilfully as he used sword or lance.

Horses of the Conquest — Conquistador speared by Indians.

The expedition landed at the mouth of the Tabasco river, and the first thing was to disembark the horses. Bernal Diaz does not say exactly how many days they had been aboard the ships. It must have been at least ten days or a fortnight, for the ships sailed slowly and they had put off time at the island of Cozumel, and other places. Once landed, the horses were so stiff that they could hardly move, and had at once to be turned loose to graze. A curious sight, this first landing of horses on the mainland of the New World, must have presented.

In some cove where there were grass and water handy, the ships rode at anchor.

High-pooped, low-waisted vessels with many little cannons, nearly all breechloaders, their forecastles balancing their poops, their tops like little forts upon the masts, the great stern lantern, right aft, and over all the Spanish ensign with its castles and its lions, hanging down listlessly in the tropic air, or fluttering in the breeze. The horses grazing, hobbled or sidelined, for it would have been madness to let them entirely loose, must have made a strange and unfamiliar note of colour as they grazed for the first time in the New World, where they were destined to multiply in countless numbers at no distant date.

The soldiers lounging about the tents, or bathing in the surf, must have been almost as stiff from long confinement and exposure in the ships as were their horses. The trees, plants, flowers, insects and the birds were all new to them. Ceibas with their long grape-like clusters of pale lilac flowers, huge, bulbous trunks and knotted roots rising above the surface of the ground, as if they were some prehistoric monsters striving to be free, appeared to menace them. Ropes of lianas, binding the trees together, crowning them after their deathly embrace with red and blue or yellow flowers; the floating ribbons of Spanish moss that flowed down from the boughs; all, everything, was strange, as strange as were the animals to Adam, when in the paradise upon the Tigris, chief glory of the Book of Genesis, he gave them names. Next day, when the horses had fed and rested, Cortés had them all saddled, and breastplates hung with hawks-bells fixed to their saddles to terrify the Indians, when they charged. He then addressed his men, giving them advice that if it had been better followed would in the future have saved many of their lives. It was to charge with shortened lances, held high. Never to spear the Indians through the body, but in their faces or their throats. His reason was, that when they drove their lances through the body, as life is very strong in Indians, it often happened that the man transfixed, seized the spear with his hands, and either pulled it from the rider's grasp, or else gave time for other Indians to rush in and kill the horseman or his horse, before he had had time to drag his lance back from the dying Indian's ribs. What Cortés wanted them to do was to turn their wrists after spearing an Indian, as a man does in tent pegging after he has lifted the peg on the point of his lance.

So all-important were the horses that Bernal Diaz specially enumerates all these soldiers (they were but thirteen in all) fit to be entrusted with a horse.

Pedro de Alvarado, Puertocarrero and Francisco de Montejo were gentlemen and knights, and as they had their own horses, of course were mentioned in the list. Alonso de Avila had no horse, so Cortés gave him the horse belonging to Ortiz el Musico and Bartolomé Garcia, "for neither of the two could ride." Juan Velazquez de Léon and Francisco de Morla also had horses allotted to them, as well as "Lares El buen Ginete" and Gonzalo Dominguez, both fine horsemen.

So all-important were the horses to the Conquistadores that Bernal Diaz gives this description of them, with their colours, merits and demerits, before he penned any of his inimitable pictures of the conquerors, even of Cortés himself.

Nor was his estimate of their importance exaggerated. Hardly had they landed when it became apparent that to work an atmosphere of terror amongst the Indians their breastplates with the jingling hawksbells, their unfamiliar air of animals from an unknown world, their speed, size, fiery eyes, their iron shoes, and the strange figures on their backs, half-sheathed in plate, and the doubt whether horse and man formed one ferocious beast, rendered them terrible to men to whom they must have seemed supernatural.

In the first skirmish, "as the ground was flat, the riders all good horsemen and some of the horses swift and well-bitted, they had the opportunity to lance (the Indians) at their pleasure, a thing convenient at the time."

Convenient at the time is a good phrase, without the least trace of hypocrisy. "After we had routed them . . . we all dismounted under a group of trees, and gave great thanks to God and to His Blessed Mother, raising our hands to heaven for giving us the day."

No doubt the God of Battles was well pleased with the thanks. As to His Blessed Mother, it leaves one puzzled. Perhaps as is to be observed in husbands and in wives, who grow more like each other by long contact, it may have been that the two personages who Bernal Diaz mentions, took the thanks so sincerely and so simply offered under the group of trees as nothing but their due.

Eight horses were wounded in this the first skirmish in which horses figured in the New World.

Diaz says, "the wounded horses we cured with grease from the dead Indians, and these were opened to get the grease from their insides." "Where the horsemen passed," he says, "there were dead lying thick and others wounded and complaining of their wounds." The dead numbered about eight hundred, mostly killed by the horsemen, for he says, "we could do little till the horsemen came upon the field." The Indians they had to face were strong athletic men, their bows so strong that not a Spaniard in the expedition could pull the string up to his ear. They shot so strongly that their arrows several times passed through a horse and remained sticking in the ground. Although the Spaniards wore a good deal of armour, and all buff coats, despite the fact of the great difference in weapons, cross-bows and swords and steel tipped lances, the Indians stood up to them manfully.

Only the horses, and they alone, inclined the victory to the Spanish side. Their strangeness and the fact that Bernal Diaz especially alludes to, that the Indians thought horse and man formed one ferocious beast, gave them the victory, for which they thanked the Deity, beneath the group of trees. Diaz perceived this clearly, for after chronicling the fact that the wounded horses had their wounds dressed with Indians' fat, he mentions casually that the wounded men had their wounds cured, either by fire, or by the Indians' grease. Not in the fight alone were their horses useful to the Conquistadores. In order to strike terror into the Indians' hearts, Cortés had recourse to a well-known stratagem. In camp upon the River of Grejalva, in the province of Tabasco, he made Ortiz de Musico, whose horse was "muy rixoso," tie him up near a mare. Then having caused the mare to be led out of sight, behind some trees, the horse commenced to neigh and stamp his feet upon the ground. The Indians were terrified at the noise he made and in especial of his fiery eyes and thought he wished to fly up and devour them. When Cortés saw their state of terror, he dismounted and taking Ortiz's horse by the bit, made as if he spoke to him. Turning to his intrepeter Aguilar, he bade him tell the Indians he had told the horse to do no harm to them. Then prudently he had him led out of sight, so that the Indians should not find out the trick.

In the next skirmish Cortés had his horse killed under him. "He bought," Diaz says, "or they gave him another called El Arriero." This horse was a dark chestnut, and had belonged to Ortiz the musician, and Bartolomé Garcia El Minero, and was one of the best in the expedition. Garcia had probably been a miner, but anyhow he and his dark chestnut are preserved for ever in the great gallery of horses and of men that Diaz probably knew well enough that he was painting for posterity.

Upon the march the soldiers talked of the tactics they should pursue. Their favourite method was to attack in threes, taking good care to hold their lances short, keeping the points high, so as to wound the Indians in the face, and to avoid their lances being pulled out of their hands. Further on upon the road to Mexico, the Indians killed a good mare belonging to Pedro de Moron. They cut off her head and sent it round to their villages to show that she was mortal. Her shoes they offered to one of their idols. This was almost sacrilege in the eyes of Bernal Diaz. Whilst he laments the death of Pedro de Moron, who died of his wounds a few days afterwards, though a good rider, his loss was not so grievous as that of the good mare.

In the preliminary skirmishes with the Tlaxcalans before Cortés was able to conclude the alliance with them against their hereditary enemies, the Mexicans, to which he owed so much of his success, the horses were the chief source of victory to the Spaniards. As time went on the Indians grew better accustomed to them and saw that they were mortal, as were their riders who at first they had looked at as the children of the sun. What the Mexicans thought of the horsemen and how they saw them is to be seen from the curious paintings in the Codex Mexicanus, fortunately preserved at Rome. How it escaped the destruction wantonly meted out by ignorant barbarians, unaware that the manuscripts contained the history of the people, is almost a miracle. Religious fervour in those days ran high, and few could tolerate the existence of other idols than those forged by themselves. During the siege of Mexico, the horses did not play so prominent a part. But in the celebrated retreat known as La Noche Triste when

Cortés was forced to abandon his new conquest for a time, many a good soldier and many a wounded man owed his life to his horse.

The horses, Bernal Diaz chronicles, had no small part all unknown to themselves in riveting the chains of slavery upon the Mexicans. Whether it was better that a whole polity, interesting by its growth, autochthonous and far removed from any other known to the older world, should be destroyed, and a fair country drenched in blood, in order that the cross should rise triumphant over the foundations of the great Teocalli, and that a civilisation whose archtype is the Bowery of New York, I leave to theologians to decide.

Innocent instruments of Allah's will, the horses had and deserved their chroniclers in Bernal Diaz, the Inca Garcilaso de la Vega and Cortés himself. Although the Inca Garcilaso has preserved the best accounts of what the horses of the conquest actually performed, giving the distances they covered upon several occasions, Diaz and he alone writes of them as friends and comrades. After the Noche Triste, when every horse was wounded and many killed, he writes, "It was the greatest grief to think upon the horses, and the valiant soldiers we had lost."

In this great retreat Cortés lost more than three hundred men and twenty horses. All the surviving horses were wounded more or less.

Once more, upon their lamentable retreat, beset on all sides both by canoes – for they retreated over a raised stone causeway to gain the land across the lake – without provisions and with increasing hordes of Indians pressing on them, those that survived once more owed their salvation "to the horses, after God." The wounded rode upon the horses who were unfit to go into the fighting, or clutched their manes and tails, "the horses that were soundest were in the front" (says Diaz), "some on our flank, some on the other side of the retreating force." When they had reached a place of safety in Tlaxcala they found that more than twelve hundred of their native allies were killed, four hundred Spaniards, more or less, were slain, and of the horses only twelve survived.

After a year's rest Cortés, who had received reinforcements, both of men and horses, advanced again on Mexico. As they fought step by step along the causeways on the lake, from their canoes the Indians killed many of their horses, spearing them with lances made of swords taken from the dead Spaniards, stuck upon canes. Cortés himself escaped being carried off for sacrifice by the devotion of his

men. He rode that day "a good dark brown horse called El Romo."
This horse either because it was too fat, or tired, as it had had but little
exercise, suddenly failed him. The enemy who was in force seized on
Cortés and dragged him to the ground. They did not kill him, for
above all things they liked to sacrifice the prisoners to Huichilobos,
their God of War. Three of his captains and some Tlaxcalan Indians
rushed to his aid, passing as Bernal Diaz says, "through a little too
much of spears and arrows and stones slung from a sling." One
Cristobal de Oli set Cortés on his horse, though badly wounded in
the head. Oli soon was wounded and both he and his leader would
have been killed had not Pedro de Alvarado, and others rushed
furiously upon the Indians. Oli was bathed in blood, and Alvarado's
horse was wounded. Diaz describes these fights so faithfully, in such
Homeric style, that after reading him one knows Cortés and his chief
captains better perhaps than we can ever know even our closest
friends. The horses, too, we know as well or better than our own, at
least in England where a man has little real companionship with the
high-priced, well-groomed and stabled animal that others feed and
care for, and he rides at the most three or four hours a day and then
sees led off to be washed and dressed by grooms. Some of the little
sketches Diaz had left of horses are inimitable, but he has put out his
full power in the portrait that he gives of Motilla, perhaps the
completest portrait of a horse that ever has been penned. We know
Motilla even better than the bright bay with four white legs and
crinkly mane who turns his head towards Spinola in Velazquez's
masterpiece, the Lances. Motilla belonged to Captain Gonzalo de
Sandoval. He was the best and fastest horse and the best bitted, for he
turned as well on one side as the other, and men said they had never
seen a better either in the Indies or in Spain. "His colour was a dark
bay, with a white star upon his forehead, and his near forefoot white.
He was called Motilla. Now when men talk of horses they say he was
as good, or almost as good, as Motilla." The Conquistadores, when
they had taken Mexico, were in two minds whether with the golden
sun and silver moon, the emeralds and the feather cloaks, they ought
to send Motilla to the Emperor Charles V. If they had done so no
doubt Charles, in his character of a Prince of Light Horsemen, would
have prized the gift. In another place Diaz said the Emperor had
heard of Motilla and his merits. Yuste would have been a worthy
burial place for Motilla had he been sent to Charles. Under the

chestnut trees in La Vega de Plasencia the greatest man and the best horse of the age would have found fitting resting-places.

Diaz has also left a fine portrait of Sandoval, the best horseman of the Conquest, and Motilla's master: "Captain Gonzalo de Sandoval" (he says) "was a brave man, and he would be about two and twenty years of age when he came to Mexico . . . He was of a good stature and well-proportioned, of reasonable size and muscular; his chest was full and broad, as were his shoulders, and his legs a little bowed. His face was rather full, and his hair and beard were chestnut-coloured. His voice was not very clear, and he lisped a little. He was not a learned man, although well-educated, nor was he anxious to get gold, but chiefly careful of his duty as a good captain. In all the wars that we had in the New Spain he always took great care of his soldiers and helped and favoured them. Rich clothes he never wore, but dressed quite plainly as befits a soldier. The Emperor mourned him for he had notice of his generous personality."

Both Motilla and Sandoval were lucky in their chronicler. The best horse and the finest horseman who went to the Conquest, will never be forgotten as long as men are moved by gallant deeds, love a good horse, and can appreciate a vigorous and homely style, couched in a Castilian that time but renders mellower, as it improves good wine.

In 1562, Hernando de Soto, one of the most sympathetic of the conquistadores, set out with reinforcements for Pizarro, for the conquest of Peru; the little town of Barcarrota in the province of Badajoz and district of Caceres was his birthplace. Thus, like the greater part of the Conquistadores, he was from Estremadura, the province that was almost left without inhabitants in those days, as so many Estremenians flocked to the conquest of the New World, drawn there by their adventurous spirit and the fact that both Pizarro and Cortés were their fellow-countrymen.

In Panama, in Nicaragua, and on the coast of Castillo de Oro, Soto learned the rudiments of a conqueror's trade. Oviedo says he was brought up "in the bad school of Pedrarias Davila in the destruction of the Indians of Castillo del Oro, graduated in the deaths of the inhabitants of Nicaragua, and canonised in Peru, according to the order of the Pizarros."

Tracking and following up a trail must have been as second nature to him. In 1532 he joined what Oviedo styles the university of the Pizarros, coming to Peru, when they were hard pressed by the

Peruvians. Arrived at Tumbez he was met by the Bishop Don Fray Vicente de Valverde, and by Gonzalo Pizarro, one of the finest horsemen "who passed to the Indies."

Waiting to disembark his men, Soto, the Bishop, and Pizarro were obliged to sit all night fully armed upon their horses in the pouring rain, awaiting an attack. Thus he made his entry to Peru in danger of his life and suffering hardship from the first day of his arrival in the land. As in the conquest of Mexico the horses played a prominent part. The Indians, far less warlike than the Mexicans, were more terrified, if possible, of the unfamiliar beasts. Although the Peruvian Indians in the main were far from warlike, then, yet they did not want courage of a passive kind.

What Soto learned in Nicaragua was no doubt to tie his horse up properly, so that the knot neither ran hard, or slipped; to mount all in one motion, not dwelling on the stirrup with his leg poised in the air, after the style of riding-schools, and not to fling himself off his horse in dismounting, as if he thought the animal was made of wood.

At his first interview with the Inca Atahualpa, Soto who must have forgotten for the moment that he was a gentleman, charged up to the throne at full gallop, checking his horse so near the Inca that it snorted in his face. Atahualpa sat as solid as a rock, though it was the first time that he had ever seen a horse. Then Soto remembered who he was and dismounting made a deep bow, after the Spanish style, and told the Inca the business that he had come about.

The episode does not show Soto in a too favourable light. Still he must have looked a gallant figure thus riding into history, lance in hand, no doubt "à la gineta" in the Spanish-Moorish style. At the siege of Cuzco Soto bore himself with courage, and was in extreme danger of his life. His share of the loot amounted to one hundred and four score thousand ducats. So he returned to Spain rich and perhaps respected, for riches though they induce servility, rarely command respect.

Still, Soto had more to recommend him than those riches that so often make a man ridiculous. He was the only Spaniard of position who protested against the base murder of the Inca Atahualpa by the Pizarro brothers.

Pizarro sent him on an expedition to the Sierra de Vilcaza mainly to get rid of him. At the head of his troops in his high Moorish saddle he leaped his horse over all the ditches on the road. The Indians marvelled and wondered if he and his horse formed but one whole.

Soto left Peru not long after the sack of Cuzco (1533). On his return to Spain he married the daughter of Pedrarias Davila. The lady was reputed to be of great beauty. This may have been so, or again it may have been alleged against her, because she was marrying a rich man. Conquest burned in Soto's blood, and he was not content to stay at home and watch his arteries grow hard.

In 1537 he entered into an agreement (*asiento*) with Charles V to conquer Florida. His Caesarean Majesty made him his Captain-General in Florida. It was a privilege that it cost Charles nothing to confer, for the country was unknown, unconquered and inhabited by ferocious Indians.

Charles also conferred a marquisate upon him. History does not record how much he paid for it, but it must have been a good round sum, for then, as now, titles were freely bought and sold.

The Caesar always drove hard bargains with such men as Soto, the Pizarros, Cortés and all those who came with empires in their hands to offer him.

When the fleet was ready Soto put to sea in a galleon called the Saint Christopher, and crossed the bar at San Lucar on the 6th of April, 1538.

He put on board more than a hundred horses. Two of them Garcilaso mentions. The first was Aceituno, Soto's favourite horse. He was the best horse in the fleet. The other belonged to Gonçalo de Silvestre, a dark chestnut, good in extreme.

Garcilaso does not omit to say that horse and rider came from Herrera de Alcantara. This is as it should be and shows the Inca understood that the dark chestnut was as much a Conquistador as was his master, and deserved honourable mention in the roll of fame.

In which particular ship Aceituno was embarked is for a wonder unnoted by the garrulous horse-loving Inca. However, Soto, who as a horseman knew the value of the master's eye, probably had him in his own ship, the St. Christopher.

The fleet made Santiago de Cuba in a little less than two months, an average passage in those days.

Soto's arrival was fêted with bull-fights and cane-play (juegos de cañas), and these the Inca says served to show him how fiery and how suitable for war the horses of the islands were.

These in the space of five and thirty years since the first conquest had multiplied enormously. The Spaniards settled in the island bred them especially to sell to conquerors going to the wars, both in Peru and Mexico. They were of course descended from the famous breed of Cordoba, long since extinct. The breed is said to have been formed during the Arab Caliphate in Cordoba, by four sires bought from the Yemen or the Hejaz, crossed with the native mares. To-day the horses born from Spanish stock in Cuba have become small and weedy by interbreeding, and certainly do not appear fiery, and still less fit for war.

At Santiago, Soto was joined by a rich man, one Vasco Porcallo de Figueroa, past fifty years of age. Soto named him at once lieutenant-general of the army and the fleet, which office he had at that time in his own hands.

Though middle-aged the new recruit was a gallant cavalier, whose love of new conquests and adventure advancing years had failed to tame. He brought a present of fifty horses, and had a host of Indians and of negroes and six and thirty horses for his household and himself. Soto with this addition and his purchases in Santiago, joined to the horses he had brought from Spain, had more than three hundred horses broken and fit for war. This was the largest force of cavalry that had set out for any conquest.

In August, 1538, Soto started for the Habana, marching in troops of fifty, leaving an interval of a week between each troop, so that they should not eat up all the provisions of the road. This was a prudent move on his part, and shows how leisurely the conquests were conducted, for time was the commodity the Conquistadores had to spare. As Soto set out from Santiago at the end of August, 1538, and took till April of the next year to reach the Habana, two hundred and fifty leagues away, he did not spare his treasure in the way of time. On May 30th, 1539, the fleet cast anchor in a bay in Florida, that Soto named after the Holy Ghost.

Whether the name continues and the bay is still named after the Holy Spirit that dull human eyes only have perceived typified as a white dove, is to the writer quite unknown. It ought to be, for surely none more beautiful could have been devised. Perhaps dour sectaries, who only use the name of Jesus as an oath, or fear to utter it, alleging that to do so would be failing in respect, have hit upon a better, and the bay new named and purged of Popery is called after some pilgrim father of old days, or modern senator. Bay of the Holy Ghost, or Hiram Beeswanger's Harbour, or by whatever appellation it is known to-day, it served as a good landing-place for Soto's cavalry. Three hundred horses must have required considerable pasturage. The conquest of Florida was to prove in a measure more difficult than those of either of the great empires of Peru and Mexico. In the first place there was nothing definite to conquer. The Indians lived in isolated villages and were as fierce and warlike as any in the New World. They proved by far the strongest bowmen that the Spaniards had encountered, and as the country was well-wooded had less to fear from cavalry. The campaign began disastrously for the horses and it was lucky for him that Soto had so many in reserve.

At the town of Tascaluça, the chief came out to greet the Spaniards, accompanied by his bodyguard. A true son of Anak he towered above his men. Soto in the same manner as Cortés appeared to think that to mount the chief upon a horse would be the greatest honour in his power to pay.

No horse in all the army, though there were over three hundred to select among, could bear the giant's weight. At last when a stout baggage animal was found, the chieftain's feet dangled upon the ground. Oviedo does not pretend, as did Cortés, that the Indian enjoyed his ride.

Indeed he says with the saving gift of humour (rare in historians), that the chief could not have been much pleased, "because the Indians looked upon those animals as if they had been lions or tigers, and feared them mightily."

At Manvila, which some say was Mobile, Soto discovered the only fortified village that any of the Conquistadores found in Florida. It was surrounded by a stout stockade, and flanked by several low wooden towers, and contained nearly ten thousand inhabitants.

At this place Soto fell into an ambush, and at one blow lost eighty of his best men and five and thirty horses, "who were no less mourned and wept for than were the men, for they saw that in them was the greatest strength of the army.

So rapid and unsuspected was the attack that the horsemen had not time to mount. Only a few gained their saddles, and these cut their way through the thickest of the Indian ranks and saved their horses and themselves. The others turned their horses loose to let them try and gallop off, or had to stand and watch them slaughtered at their lines, the Indians shooting them, with as great eagerness as they shot the men.

Soto in a furious charge cleared the town of Indians, only to find that in the process of the fight, his baggage and provisions had been carried off or burned. This left him in a desperate plight, for his men had but the clothes they wore and the arms they carried in their hands. This reverse brought about the failure of the expedition, though Soto struggled on in the face of every difficulty.

Nothing from that moment prospered with him, though he displayed his usual gallantry. It was now three years since the expedition had sailed from Cuba and he had lost more than a hundred horses and two hundred men. The Indians used their bows so skilfully and with such strength that upon several occasions their arrows pierced a horse and stuck into the ground.

In 1541 the Indians attacked him in his winter quarters, and that so suddenly that many of his soldiers turned and fled.

The rout might have become general had not Nuño Tovar, a gallant captain, whose aspect was so terrible that oftentimes the Indians turned and fled at the mere sight of him on his fine black horse risen to the occasion.

Springing upon his horse and galloping before the fugitives, just as a gaucho or a cowpuncher rides, when cattle run before a storm, he called out, "Where do you run to? Do you think the walls of Cordoba or Seville are at hand to shelter you?"

When Soto heard the alarm he mounted hastily and charged the Indians, followed but by a page or two and by a company of Portuguese, all of whom had served in the frontier wars of Africa. Charging in front "with the desire to kill an Indian who had been foremost in the fight," and bearing hard on his off stirrup, the saddle turned and he was left defenceless on the ground. His peril was extreme, for as he always slept in his clothes, he had but put a helmet on and with his shield and lance, jumped on his horse without defensive armour, so that had not a page called Tapia set him on his horse, he would have perished at the Indian's hands. The rout was stopped and victory gained at a great price, for the Indians set fire to the straw shelters that served as stables, and more than eighty of their best horses were either shot as they stood feeding at their mangers, or perished in the flames.

Right to the end of the disastrous expedition, the horses were the trump card in Soto's hand. Dead, their hides provided rough jackets for the soldiers, or taken off entire were fashioned into coracles to cross the rivers. Even after Soto's death when few of them were left, they played their part, for mounting them the soldiers galloped backwards and forwards over his grave, so that the Indians should not see where it had been dug.

The Inca Garcilaso has preserved by far the fullest accounts of what the horses of those days were able to perform. In Soto's fleet there came one Gonçalo de Silvestre, whom he made one of his bodyguard. Born at Herrera de Alcantara in the province of Caceres, he was but twenty years of age when he set out from Spain. When they arrived in Florida, Soto sent off Captain Balthasar de Gallegos to explore the land and send him a report. Charmed with the natural beauty of the country, its trees and shrubs, "as walnuts, figs and mulberries, with plums and pears and oak, and others which we do not know, either in Old or New Castile," he sent off four on horseback, to tell his leader he was resting at a certain chieftain's village and there was food enough there to suffice the army for several days.

One of the four was Gonçalo de Silvestre, who though a youth must have been known already as a horseman. The four on horseback in two days made five and twenty leagues, not a bad record in a country, such as Florida, set thick with swamps and on a road quite unfamiliar to the hard-riding four. Fresh from a voyage of several months, ridden by men whose weapons, armour and their cloaks together with the Moorish saddle, must have brought up the weight they had to carry to at least sixteen stone, upon rough tracks, the horses showed at their first trial that they were fit for conquerors to ride. The tracks must have been very rough or non-existent, the riders riding by the sun, and the food unfamiliar, for bred on barley, the horses had to accustom themselves to maize, and do hard work, at once on the new food.

This gallop was the first of many in which Gonçalo Silvestre proved himself one of the most intrepid scouts and tireless horsemen of any of the Conquistadores of America. When Soto's expedition arrived at a great swamp, which he says was a league across, full of mud and very difficult to cross, eight days his scouts laboured to find a ford, or some way of getting round. At last, with about a hundred men he crossed it, but found himself without supplies and cut off

from the main body of his army for the bulk of the expedition had
moved but little from the coast.

Soto cast about for a fitting messenger, and having called Gonçalo
Silvestre to him, he said, "Fortune has given you the best horse in the
army, but it was only that you should work the more." He told him
to choose his own companion, and to start at once, adding that if the
Indians were to catch him in the swamp, his life would not be worth a
pin. "Although the road may seem to you both long and arduous, I
know (he said) to whom I commit the task."

The food that Soto sent for was Spartan in its simplicity, consisting
of ship biscuits, and cheese. Gonçalo, without answering a word,
mounted his horse and set out for the camp.

Upon the road he met a friend of his, Juan Lopez Cacho, one of the
general's pages, who hailed from Seville, and was just twenty years of
age.

Gonçalo said to him, "The general commands that you are to go
with me back to the camp, therefore follow me at once." Juan Lopez
Cacho answered saying he was tired and could not go. Then did
Gonçalo blurt out the truth, a thing most men, if they are prudent,
usually decline to do, till they can see advantage in it. "The
Governor," he said, "told me to choose a comrade, and it is you I
choose. Therefore, if you will come, come in God's name, and if you
will not come, then in the same name stay."

Thus saying, he spurred his horse and struck into the trail, and
Cacho, though unwillingly, mounted his horse and followed him.

Those who have ridden on such errands, know how they must
have felt as, turning in their saddles, they took a last look at the camp
fires, before they rode into the night.

The journey that they set out upon is perhaps the most remarkable
of any of the recorded rides of the whole conquest of America. Of it,
and of it alone, are distances recorded, and all the minutiae of frontier
life during a ride through hostile Indian territory, set down by one
who was as familiar with the lance as with the pen. In the various
histories of the conquest, written as they often were by men who had
served either as officers or in the ranks, feats of individual horses are
recorded, but in the record of Silvestre's ride alone it becomes
possible to form an estimate of what the horses of the conquest were.
In the first place the two young men were riding light, with probably
but a cheese and a few biscuits in their saddle-bags. Corn for their

horses they had none, therefore the ride was done on grass-fed horses, that had but recently come off a long sea voyage, and had not had the time to get accustomed to a climate far different from that of Spain.

For the first five leagues, the trail ran through the plains, and thus they rode in safety, for the way was clear of streams, of hills, of woods, or of any place in which an ambush could be laid. But as they neared the swamp, the peril was so great that nothing which they could have done would have availed them, "had not the Lord Himself helped them on their way, showing His power by putting in the horses' heads the instinct to find out the surest track."

These horses, moved either by their natural instinct, or by the intervention of a higher power, set themselves to retrace the road by which they had been brought, following it up "like hounds or pointers," with their noses trailing on the ground.

It was well they did so, for it is difficult at night for Christians to follow up a trail, though they can read and write and cypher, and are endowed with faith, sufficient to make plain all miracles. At the beginning, with the lack of instinct natural to man, who as a general rule dissipates most of the gifts he has received from nature by what he thinks is education, the riders pulled the reins, thinking perhaps to keep their mounts from stumbling, or to direct them on the trail. The horses took no notice, which inclines one to believe that they were really guided from on high, and did not answer to the bit. They still kept on upon the trail, going as straight as if they had an invisible pole star to direct them, and snorting loudly now and then. Gonçalo's horse was the better tracker of the two, in following the trail, and finding it again, wherever it grew faint. The Inca says that was not wonderful, nor should the reader marvel at the fact, "for both by markings and colour he was naturally formed, in peace and war, to be extreme in everything."

Was he not chestnut of the darkest shade, almost the colour of pitch? His near fore foot was white, and he had a blaze upon his face that came so far down on his nose that he appeared to drink it. All these are signs by which a Spanish horseman of those days knew a good horse. They gave sure promise both of loyalty and bottom in horses, whether hacks or chargers, in which they might prevail. Juan Lopez Cacho's horse was a fox-coloured chestnut, with black points and tail, and although good exceedingly, not quite the equal of the other horse, who all the night guided his master and his friend.

Gonçalo having understood the intention and the goodness of his horse, let him do as he liked, without restraining him, and thus the night wore on, and the two friends still kept upon their way. With all these difficulties and others which it is easier to imagine than to write about, the two young men kept on, half dead with hunger and with cold. For the last two days their food had been only some ears of maize, which grain the Indians sowed in fertile places and left to ripen, coming to harvest it when it was ripe. Sleep gained upon them and upon their horses, who for their part were hungry, having been saddled for the past two days with but their bridles off for a moment now and then to give them water, and let them crop a little grass.

As they passed through the woods, upon the right hand and the left, they saw the fires of Indian camps.

"Those Gentiles danced and drank, keeping some feast of theirs, and though the dogs barked loudly the Lord Himself stopped up the Indians' ears," so that they did not hear their dogs, or the clinking of the armour as the horses trotted on the trail. Juan Lopez Cacho who had started tired from the camp, pulled up his horse and said that he must sleep. "Only a minute let us sleep," he said, "or if not, run your lance through my body and end my misery."

Gonçalo who had twice refused to let him sleep, now lost his patience, and replied "Sleep then in an unlucky hour (en hora mala) and lose our lives – for if the sun rises whilst we are on the road, the Indians will soon see us and our lives be lost."

Juan Lopez Cacho had no sooner heard Gonçalo's words, than he let himself slide out of the saddle to the ground, and instantly was wrapped in sleep as if he had been dead. Gonçalo took his lance and sat upon his horse, holding the other by the reins. A sudden darkness overspread the sky and then a rain descended like a deluge, but still Juan Lopez Cacho slept, as if he had been dead.

At the first streak of dawn, almost by magic, as it seemed, the torrents ceased and the sun rose instantly.

At the first light of dawn Gonçalo, who perhaps had dozed a little on his horse, called to his friend, knowing the danger that they ran. The wretched man was sleeping in the mud, and if he had been left alone, would without doubt have not awakened, but to feel the

Indians' arrows passing through his body, in the brief interval between sleep and death.

Gonçalo dared not speak loudly, but as the Inca says, "in a low husky voice called on his friend."

He, fast as the Seven Sleepers, did not stir, until Gonçalo beat him with his lance. Then, sitting up, he wrung the water from his hair, and slowly mounted, whilst Gonçalo cursed him, and said that for his weakness they were in peril of their lives and hardly could escape.

Even as Cacho climbed upon his horse the Indians camped not far off, saw them and raised a yell, beating on drums, blowing war whistles and sounding on the conch. At the noise they made, canoes shot out from the reedy margins of the swamp and barred their passage to the other side. So many came, the Inca says, that they appeared more like the leaves of trees that floated on the swamps, than war canoes.

The two companions, though they saw the danger, yet could not return, for to the rear the Indians had closed up upon them. So at a gallop they charged into the swamp, the Indians' arrows raining on their armour, like a very hail. But God was pleased, as both their horses were deep in the water, and their own harness was of proof, to allow them to escape unhurt.

"This they took as no small miracle, for the infinity of arrows was so great that when they turned to look upon the other side, the water was as thickly strewn with them as is a street with rushes upon the day of some solemnity or feast." When the two adventurous youths emerged all dripping on the bank, those in the army camped near the swamp heard the Indians' yells, and mounting quickly thirty or forty horsemen spurred up to the swamp.

In front of all of them rode Captain Nuño Tobár, galloping furiously upon a splendid dappled grey. His horse looked so ferocious to the Indians and he himself so gallant in his seat, that the mere sight of him caused all the Indians to retreat.

Gonçalo's work was not yet over, after his long ride. On his arrival at the camp, after having eaten two cobs of roast maize, when the convoy of food was ready, he started back to show the way across the swamp as his horse still was fresh.

Juan Lopez Cacho stayed in the camp to rest. The convoy reached the camp where Soto was in safety, and found him in a valley in which the Indians had left great crops of corn, so that the soldiers and their horses feasted abundantly, gathering the corn, cutting it as they rode, the horses snatching mouthfuls as they marched.

Soto, after a few months, having marched about a hundred and fifty leagues, as far as Apalache, found himself once more at a great distance from his base as the bulk of his forces was still camped close to the coast, at the head of a great inlet that the Inca calls All Saints.

So he determined to wait there, as corn was plentiful.

Then he chose thirty of the best horsemen and sent them back, to hurry his lieutenant Pedro Calderon, as he found winter coming on.

With these, of course, Gonçalo went on his good horse, now rested and well fed. The territory between the general and the coast was one succession of great swamps, through which ran several rivers.

Indians were thick upon the road and Indians not like those of Mexico, who trembled at the sight of horses, but warriors who drew such powerful bows that Spanish plate was as mere paper to their shafts. "He," says the Inca, "who had not Milan steel threw off his armour, as it did not protect him, and put on a quilted cotton jacket such as the Indians used, which turned an arrow better than inferior plate."

These quilted doublets were known as escaupiles, and at the conquest of Colombia, the Spaniards covered the rider from head to foot with them, even devising armour for the horse that came down to his knees.

Fray Pedro de Aguado says that a horse-soldier and his horse appeared gigantic, thus arrayed with cotton armour, but they were safe as if shut up within a tower. Upon October 20th, 1539, the thirty started, all riding lightly armed, with but their helmets and light coats of mail above their clothes. All carried lances and had saddlebags, with some rations for themselves, spare horse-shoes and nails, a hammer and all requisites for paring horses' feet.

Gonçalo had had one desperate ride. The second was to prove more desperate still, and proved him a man fit to resist all perils and all hardships.

It also served to prove the extraordinary powers of resistance of the horses that the thirty horsemen rode, whether they had come from Spain or whether they were island bred.

The thirty must have looked rather like horsemen of the Sahara below Morocco, riding as they did in the Moorish saddle with short stirrup leathers, the long Arab reins and powerful mameluke bit. Probably many of them spoke or at least understood Arabic, which was still much spoken in the country districts in the time of Charles V. It is possible, too, that some of them had served in Africa.

They left the camp at a "reasonable hour," before the heat of day, so that no word should get abroad which way they were to go. As the first march led them through a level plain, they travelled fast, galloping now and then, but in the main keeping their horses to the "Castilian pace."

The God of Battles went with them, for coming on two Indians by the way they speared them "handsomely," so that they should not raise the alarm and bring the others out upon their track. That day they made "full thirteen leagues," not a bad journey for men who had only a single horse apiece, and were not certain of the road, and that on grass-fed horses.

They passed the great swamp without adventure, and camped on the far side. Next day, before the sun was up, they left the swamp of Apalache and riding twelve good leagues, got close to Osachile, a little Indian town; fearing the Indians might attack them and with their arrows wound or disable any of the horses they waited until nightfall, and then mounting again passed through the Indian village at a gallop.

A league beyond the town they halted, and passed the remaining hours of darkness sleeping, whilst they left a third of their companions on the watch. Again that day they travelled thirteen leagues. Starting before the dawn at a fast gallop, they made five leagues, doing their best because they feared the Indians might get word beforehand of their coming, the thing which they most feared.

"We reached the river Osachile about midday" (says the chronicler), "the horses were so good that they stood everything." They must have been extraordinarily good, for though the men rode light the horses had no corn, and nothing wears a horse out more upon a journey than the want of sleep. Gonçalo was the first to reach the river; he passed it swimming on his horse, the rest all followed him, and then wet as they were sat down to breakfast, after thanking God. In four more leagues they reached the town of Vitachico, where a month before they had been in battle, fearing to find the place rebuilt, and the Indians ready to bar their way. To their astonishment nothing had been done, the charred huts were all empty and the bodies of the dead Indians lying where they had been killed.

The "thirty lances" as the Inca calls them, when they had passed the town, fell in upon the road with a pair of Indian hunters, on the search for game, their bows were in their hands, and at their backs they carried quivers full of arrows, and they had crowns of feathers on their heads. The Inca calls them "dos Indios gentiles hombres" which may have meant two Indian gentlemen, or merely two tall well-made men. Such as they were, one of them proved himself more than a gentleman, and rightly does the Inca chronicle his deed. Seeing the thirty lances suddenly, the Indian gentlemen took refuge underneath a tree. The Inca calls it "the Nogal" by which he probably meant either a hickory or a pecan.

As they were armed with bows, and as the Spaniards only carried lances and swords, and probably no firearms, the Indians were relatively safe as the branches of a pecan hang low. One of them taken with panic came out and ran to gain the woods. Two of the "lances" galloped after him, not heeding all their captain's cries to stop. They caught up the poor devil and speared him, a feat the Inca rightly says was not difficult for two well mounted men. The other Indian gentleman was of another breed.

As the Spaniards approached the tree, galloping fast to avoid his arrows, he turned his bow on each one as he passed, but took good care never to shoot. Thus, many a frontiersman has saved his life when caught alone upon the plains, by getting off his horse and standing with his rifle resting on the saddle, pointing it at the Indians as they gallop round him, not daring to approach.

To fire and miss is fatal, and for the Indians to rush in is certain death for some of them. So did it fall out with the Indian underneath the tree. None of the "thirty" cared to go too near, although Gonçalo wanted to attack the man on foot. To this his captain wisely answered that the Indian's death would be of little profit to them, but that the loss or wounding of a horse would be disastrous to them all. So making a wide circle the thirty lances galloped past the tree, the Indian covering every one of them, until the last had gone. Then breaking out into a fury, he upbraided them for cowards, shouting out insults with unseemly gestures, from his post beneath the tree. That day, the third from leaving camp, the "thirty lances" galloped seventeen leagues, and on the fourth day another seventeen, with all their horses going well and strongly, playing with their bits.

Upon the evening of the fourth day, they met and speared seven or eight Indians, a fair day's sport as it would seem for men upon the road. Then coming to an open prairie they camped till midnight, and starting when the moon got up, rode five leagues more before the break of day.

This brought them to the river Ochali that they hoped to find fordable and low. Unluckily it was in flood and as they stood upon the banks deliberating, a band of Indians suddenly appeared.

Once more the lances showed their aptitude for frontier life. Their captain called on twelve of them to swim across and hold the landing-place upon the other side. Stripped to their shirts and drawers and with their coats of mail, helmets and lances in their hands, they plunged into the flood. Whilst they were swimming their comrades held the Indians in check, and others cut down boughs with which to pass the saddles, saddlebags and clothes, and several men who could not swim.

The danger was extreme, for if a band of Indians had appeared upon the further bank they could have easily shot all the swimmers, and then holding the landing-place have either shot the rest, or forced them against the ranks of the other Indians who were closing up behind. Eleven of the swimmers having crossed, they sent out scouts to watch the higher ground: the scouts naked, but for their dripping shirts and rusty coats of mail and helmets, must have looked just as wild as did the Indians. The last man of the twelve was Lopez Cacho, whose horse missing the landing-place, was carried downwards by the current, and only rescued by four good swimmers, who plunging in kept just above the tired horse to break the current, so that he gained the bank, but on the same side of the river from which he entered it.

Just as Juan Lopez Cacho and his tired horse emerged upon the bank, a band of Indians appeared and advanced on the eleven swimmers on the other side. This showed how wise their captain was, in sending to hold the landing-place. The eleven mounting half naked on their horses, charged on the Indians and forced them to retreat. The raft of boughs and branches being ready, four swimmers, after loading it with saddles and with cloaks passed to the other side, their comrades holding back the Indians by frequent charges on them. The cloaks were what the eleven on the other side most wanted, for the north wind blew cold. Those who have suffered in its blast in Texas and in Florida, can estimate how inadequate a dress, a helmet and a shirt of mail over a dripping shirt was to the shivering men. Four times the swimmers went across, the wind rising at every journey and piercing them to the bone. At last, but two were left upon the bank alone. These were Gonçalo and one Hernando Atanasio. The latter having got upon the raft, Gonçalo charged the Indians furiously and having driven them all back, instantly wheeled his horse, and coming to the bank, plunged in with saddle, bridle, and his armour, as he was. The Indians were so amazed that he gained the middle of the stream before they shot at him. The arrows at that distance rattled harmlessly against his coat of mail, and by good luck his horse escaped a wound. The Inca says the horses were so frightened of the Indians that they seemed glad to go into the icy stream. Therefore, he says, the riders taking example from them, refused no danger and in the future skirked no difficulty.

"Thus all the men and horses crossed the river Ochali, and by the help of God, neither a man nor horse was hurt."

Juan Lopez Cacho, who had been unlucky from the start, was now so tired with the exertions he had made in crossing, and had remained so long immersed and then exposed to the full force of the north wind, that he was almost frozen, and stood like a statue unable to move hand or foot. So placing him upon a horse they took him to the Indian town of Ochale, from which the Indians had retired, as soon as the "thirty lances" had arrived. Not daring to go into any of the huts, for fear of lurking enemies, and most of all for fear that any of their horses would be shot, they camped upon the square and lighted four great fires at every angle of their camp.

In front of one of them they put Juan Lopez Cacho and covering him with their cloaks, waited until he thawed. One of them found a dry shirt in his saddlebags, and it proved the finest gift he could have had.

Till nightfall they waited in the town caring for Cacho whom they determined on no account to leave, although delay should cost them all their lives. They knew that if he could not manage to sit his horse by nightfall the Indians would have time to muster and attack in force. All day they fed their horses upon Indian corn, and though the town contained much fruit and vegetables, took nothing for themselves, but maize, with which they filled their saddlebags, reflecting that it served as food both for their horses and themselves. So well they travelled that by daylight they had made six leagues. If they met any Indians on the road they speared them incontinently, so that they might not carry news. When they passed desert country, they walked their horses, but yet made such good speed that in that day they travelled nearly twenty leagues (sixty miles), a wonderful march after the hard work the horses had had during the five preceding days. Upon the seventh day, they started early and after a few hours upon the road, one Pedro de Atiença fell ill, and in an hour or two died, still seated on his horse. His fellow riders buried him, digging his grave with the axes, which they had for breaking firewood. They dug his grave as speedily as possible, some of them holding the horses, whilst the others dug. Then they remounted, "half amazed at having left a comrade dead and buried, who but an hour ago was riding by their side." At sunset they arrived close to the pass, in the Great Swamp, having once more done twenty leagues, with the time included that they had lost in burying their friend.

In what condition poor Juan Lopez Cacho found himself after his ride of sixty miles, fastened upon his horse, the Inca does not say. That night they could not sleep, the cold was so intense. The horses must have suffered terribly, for in such cold there could have been nothing for them to eat except the maize that they had put up in their saddlebags. They made great fires and whilst a third kept watch, the others tried to sleep. Towards midnight they were all awakened for one Juan de Soto, worn out with the hardships and the cold, died, almost without a word. One of the company who had become light-headed with the want of sleep and food, ran violently into the darkness, shouting out, "Plague, the plague has come upon us." But one of those who had remained before the fire, called Gomez Arias, called to him saying, "The plague we have, comes from the journey and the want of food. From this you cannot fly. Here is not Seville, or its Axarafe, or the Arenal."

This was self-evident, and the man returning joined in the prayers they put up for their dead comrade's soul. With this help for their troubles they passed the night.

Day broke with an intensely cold north wind, but luckily the water in the swamp was lower than it had been at night. What all most feared was that the Indians should come in their canoes to stop their passage, for they had neither firearms nor crossbows with which to keep them off.

Luckily for them no Indians appeared, although the day proved arduous enough. Placing eight of the company who could not swim, upon a sort of raft, together with the saddles, lances and the cloaks, they passed them over, and then tried to make the horses cross.

Nothing would make them face the icy cold, and the rest who could swim had to take off their clothes and tying ropes to the horses swim and pull them after them. After three hours of struggling, in the water, none of the horses could be induced to face the water and the cold.

At last the horse of Gonçalo Silvestre and another passed, but still the rest were obstinate, although the swimmers hauled upon the ropes, and those upon the bank beat them with sticks and shouted at them.

The unlucky men were blue with cold and looked like corpses as they shivered on the bank when they came out to rest.

All the time that they struggled some of them kept guard, seated upon their horses with their lances in their hands. A gleam of sun at midday warmed the water, and at last all of the horses were got across. They and their riders were so benumbed with cold and so worn out with their exertions they could hardly stand upon their feet. So having made large fires they camped upon the plain, the fierce north wind rendering sleep impossible. No doubt the night was long enough, for they were almost starving, for all the corn they still had in their saddlebags they gave the horses, for in them lay the only hope of safety, after God's providence.

Once more the first light saw them on the road, their company reduced by two. The horses of the dead men, saddled as they were, accompanied them, running beside them, and occasionally taking the lead, as if they followed up a trail. Perhaps they did so, as the army had once passed along the road that they were travelling, and no animal in a wild country can better find its way than can a horse. That day their march was thirteen leagues.

Next morning about an hour before day broke, the half-breed Pedro Moron who had the keenest sense of smell in all the Indies, suddenly stopped and said, "I smell a fire."

A league upon the road they came upon a camp of Indians sitting round a fire and busily engaged in roasting fish. Charging the fire, "the thirty" scattered them, and though the horses galloped through the camp and all the fish were strewed upon the sand, the riders were so hungry that without washing it, they straight devoured them all.

After a five leagues' march, the horse of Lopez Cacho tired and nothing they could do would make it keep up with the rest. So taking off the saddle and hanging it upon a tree, they left him grazing, grieving as for a comrade, for they felt sure that the first Indian who saw him would put an arrow through him, "for the Indians feared the horses like the plague."

Juan Lopez Cacho had by this time recovered, and after taking off the bridle from his horse mounted one of the horses of the dead men, and once again the company set out.

By this time only six leagues remained to cover, and their hearts began to rise. They galloped wearily until within a league or two of Hirihigua, where Captain Pedro Calderon, with forty horse and eight foot soldiers, still lay encamped.

When they arrived close to a little lake near Hirihigua, they came upon fresh trail of horses, and in a pool saw signs of soap, where Spaniards had washed clothes.

This raised their spirits, and their horses smelling their fellows pricked up their ears and danced about – at least so says the Inca – as if they had but just left stables, for a morning ride.

An hour from sunset they came near the town, and as they gazed, a line of horsemen riding in pairs came out of the chief gate. "The Thirty" recognised them from afar, and forming into pairs, "as if they had been riding to a tournament," spurred their tired horses, and with loud shouts, entered the town, full gallop, twirling their lances round their heads.

Each couple started separately, "as is the custom in the game of Canes," and as one couple reached the gate the next one started.

So, as the Inca says, "thus terminated as at a tournament, the hardships and the perils of this eventful ride."

In eleven days, one of which they lost in crossing the Great Swamp, and one in passing the Ochali river, they had ridden one hundred and fifty leagues, and that on tracks but just discernible, with both their horses and themselves half starved, and all the time in such dire peril, "that their lives hung upon a thread such as a spider weaves."

On the third day after they reached the town, some friendly

Indians brought in the tired horse that Lopez Cacho had left grazing underneath the trees. The saddle and the bridle they carried on their heads, as none of them had dared to put them on the horse.

Their ride was over, and it remains a marvel, taking all things into consideration, the want of food, the cold, the weight the horses bore, for with their saddles á la gineta, their coats of mail, their helmets, lances, axes, and the corn they carried in their saddlebags, none of them could have ridden under sixteen stone, and some far heavier.

The want of any certain track, the passing of the Great Swamp, and of the river Ochali, in the conditions that the Inca tells of, contributed to make their ride the more extraordinary. None of the horses seemed to have suffered except the horse Juan Lopez Cacho rode, and even he was able to come into camp after a three days' rest.

Still, there was no rest either for horses or for men. Captain Pedro Calderon, set out to rejoin Soto the instant after having received the message the thirty Lances rode so gallantly to bring. All went well with them till within a short day's journey of the Great Swamp. There the Indians set upon them, and once more a man stood with his bow drawn and his arrow pointed as before. This time Silvestre was not to be restrained, and charging fiercely, ran his lance through the Indian but not before he had time to draw his bow. The arrow struck Gonçalo's horse right in the middle of the chest, and stretched him dead without a movement, so that the Indian, the rider and his horse were all upon the ground at once. So died Aceituno, Gonçalo's celebrated horse that he had brought from Spain, and who had served him gallantly throughout the celebrated ride. The soldiers (says the Inca) mourned his loss, for he was held the best not only in the army, but in the Indies at the time.

THE STATIONMASTER'S HORSE

After the long war in Paraguay, the little railway built by the tyrant Lopez, that ran from Asuncion to Paraguari, only some thirty miles, fell into a semi-ruinous condition.

It still performed a journey on alternate days, and ran, or rather staggered, along on a rough track, almost unballasted. Sleepers had been taken out for firewood, by the country people here and there, or had decayed and never been replaced. The line was quite unfenced, and now and then a bullock strayed upon it and was run down or sometimes was found sleeping on the track. Then the train stopped, if the engine-driver saw the animal in time. He blew his whistle loudly, the passengers all started, and if the bullock refused to move, got down and stoned it off the line. The bridges luckily were few, and were constructed of the hard imperishable woods so plentiful in Paraguay. They had no railings, and when, after the downpours of the tropics, the streams they crossed were flooded, the water lapped up and covered them to the depth of several inches, so that the train appeared to roll upon the waters, and gave the passengers an experience they were not likely to forget. The engine-driver kept his eyes fixed firmly on a tree or any other object on the bank, just as a man crossing a flooded stream on horseback dares not look down upon the rushing waters, but stares in front of him, above his horse's head. Overhead bridges fortunately did not exist, and there was but a single cutting in the thirty miles. It filled with water in the rains, and now and then delayed the trains a day or two, but no one minded, for time was what the people had the most of on their hands, and certainly they were not niggardly in the disposal of it.

The engines that burned wood achieved a maximum of ten miles an hour, but again no one minded, for that was greater than the speed of the bullock carts to which they had been accustomed all their lives.

Thus they looked on the railway as a marvel, and spoke of it as a sign of progress that ennobled man and made him truly only a little lower than the angels and the best beloved creation of the Deity.

Shares, dividends, balance sheets, and all the rest of the mysterious processes without which no railway in these more favoured times can run a yard, were never heard of, for the line was run by Government, who paid the salaries of the engine-drivers, who were all foreigners, when they had any cash in hand. When there was none, the officials, who had all married Paraguayan women, were left dependent on their efforts for a meal.

The telegraph, with the wires sagging like the lianas sagged from tree to tree in the great woods through which the greater portion of the line was built, was seldom in good order, so that as it stopped at the rail-head of the line, the better plan was to entrust a letter to the guard or engine-driver.

Certainly that little line through the primeval forest, with now and then breaks of open plain, dotted here and there, with the dwarf scrubby palms called yatais, was one of the most curious and interesting the world has ever known. The trains in general started an hour or two behind the time that they were supposed to start, picking up passengers like an old-time omnibus. Men standing at the corner of a wood waved coats or handkerchiefs, or in some cases a green palm leaf, to the engine-driver. He generally slowed down his impetuous career to about three miles an hour, and then the signaller, running alongside, was pulled up by a score of willing hands stretched out to him. In the case when the signaller had women with him, or a package too heavy to be thrown upon a truck in motion, the train would stop, the people scramble up, and haul their package up after them. Sometimes a man on horseback, urging his horse up to the train, with shouts, and blows of his flat-lashed "rebenque" that sounded much severer than they really were, and keeping up a ceaseless drumming of his bare heels upon its flanks, would hand a letter or a little packet to the engine-driver or to some travelling friend. At times the train appeared to stop, for no apparent reason, as nobody appeared out of the forest, either to pass the time of day or to enquire the news. Upon inclines, active young men sprinted behind the train until they caught up the last wagons; then, encouraged by the riders – for to call them "passengers" would be an unnecessary euphemism – and placing a brown hand upon the moving truck, they vaulted inboard and lay breathless for a minute, perspiring plentifully. At places such as Luque, Itá and Ipacaray, the little townships through which the harbinger of progress ran, the stops were lengthy.

Women in long white sleeveless smocks (their only garment) went about selling "chipa" – the Paraguayan bread of mandioca flour, flavoured with cheese, as indigestible as an old-fashioned Pitcaithly bannock – pieces of sugar-cane, oranges and bananas, rough lumps of dark brown sugar, done up in plantain leaves, and tasting of the lye used in their manufacture, with other delicacies called in Spanish "fruits of the country." The sun poured down upon the platform, crowded with women, for men were very scarce in Paraguay in those days. They kept up a perpetual shrill chattering in Guarani; occasionally in broken Spanish, plentifully interlarded with interjections, such as Baié pico, Iponaité, Añariu, in their more familiar tongue. Outside the station the donkeys on which the women had brought their merchandise nibbled the waving grass or chased one another in the sand. A scraggy horse or two, looking half starved and saddled with a miserable old native saddle, the stirrups often a mere knot of hide to be held by the naked toes, nodded in the fierce sun with his feet hobbled or fastened to a post. After a longer or a shorter interval, the stationmaster, generally well-dressed in white, his head crowned with an official semi-military cap, his bare feet shoved into carpincho leather slippers down at heel, and smoking a cigar, would appear upon the platform, elbow his way amongst the crowd of women, pinching them and addressing salacious compliments to those he deemed attractive, till he reached the guard or engine-driver, gossip a little with him, and signal to a female porter to ring the starting bell. This she did with a perfunctory air. The engine-driver sounded his

" a little quick to mount."

whistle shrilly, and the train, in a long series of jerks, as if protesting, bumped off from the platform in a cloud of dust.

Difference of classes may have existed, but only theoretically, like the rights of man, equality, liberty, or any of the other mendacious bywords that mankind loves to write large and disregard. No matter what the passenger unused to Paraguay paid for his ticket, the carriage was at once invaded by the other travellers, smoking and talking volubly and spitting so profusely that it was evident that no matter what diseases Paraguay was subject to, consumption had no place amongst them.

The jolting was terrific, the heat infernal, and the whole train crowded with people, who sat in open trucks, upon the tops of carriages, on footboards, or on anything that would contain them, smoking and chattering, and in their white clothes as the train slowly jolted onwards, looking like a swarm of butterflies. Certainly its progress was not speedy, but as a general rule it reached its destination, though hours behind its time.

Having to write one day from the railhead at Paraguari to Asuncion, only some thirty miles away, as the train started by a miracle at the hour that it was advertised to start, I missed it, and as the trains ran only on alternate days, the telegraph was not in working order, and no one happened to be going to the capital, someone advised me to borrow a good horse and overtake the train at some of its innumerable stoppages.

The stationmaster lent me his Zebruno, that is a cream colour, so dark as to be almost brown, with a black mane and tail, a colour that in the Argentine is much esteemed as a sure sign of a good constitution in a horse, and staying power.

He proved a little hard to mount, for he was full of corn and seldom ridden, and more than a little hard to stay upon his back for the first few minutes, a little scary, but high-couraged and as sure-footed as a mule.

I overtook the train some ten miles down the line, at a small station – Itá, if I remember rightly – after a wild ride, on a red sandy road, mostly through forest, close to the railway line, so that it was impossible to lose the track, although I did not know a yard of it.

Now and then it emerged upon the plain, and then, taking the Zebruno by the head, who by this time was settling down a little, I touched him with the spur. He answered, snorting, with a bound, and then I made good time.

I gave the letter to the engine-driver, who put it carefully into the pocket of his belt, crumpling it up so that it looked like a dead locust. Then wishing me good luck on my ride home, for night was falling, the road was almost uninhabited, tigers abounded and there was always a chance of meeting with "bad people" ("mala gente"), he cursed the country heartily, lit a cigar, spat with precision on to the track, released his lever and slid into the night.

The cream colour, who had got his second wind and rested, reared as the hind-lights passed him, and as I wheeled him, struck into a steady gallop that, as the phrase goes, "soon eats up the leagues."

A light breeze raised his mane a little and set the palm trees rustling, fireflies came out and lit the clumps of the wild orange trees, looking like spirits of disembodied butterflies as they flitted to and fro. Occasionally we – that is the cream colour and myself – had a slight difference of opinion at the crossing of a stream, when the musky scent of an unseen alligator or an ominous rustling in the thickets startled him.

As we cantered into Paraguari, he was still pulling at his bit, and nearly terminated my career in this vale of tears by a wild rush he made to get into his shed, that was too low to let a man pass underneath on horseback. I thanked the stationmaster for his horse, unsaddled him, emptied a tin mug of water over his sweating back, and threw him down a bundle of fresh Pindó leaves to keep him occupied till he was ready for his maize.

Then I strolled into the station café, where Exaltacion Medina, Joao Ferreira, and, I think, Enrique Clerici were playing billiards, whilst they waited for me.

SANTA MARIA MAYOR

The great Capilla, the largest in the Jesuit Reductions of Paraguay, was built round a huge square, almost a quarter of a mile across.

Upon three sides ran the low, continuous line of houses, like a "row" in a Scotch mining village or a phalanstery designed by Prudhon or St. Simon in their treatises; but by the grace of a kind providence never carried out, either in bricks or stone.

Each dwelling-place was of the same design and size as all the rest. Rough tiles made in the Jesuit times, but now weathered and broken, showing the rafters tied with raw hide in many places, formed the long roof, that looked a little like the pent-house of a tennis court.

A deep verandah ran in front, stretching from one end to the other of the square, supported on great balks of wood, which, after more than two hundred years and the assaults of weather and the all-devouring ants, still showed the adze marks where they had been dressed. The timber was so hard that you could scarcely drive a nail into it, despite the flight of time since it was first set up. Rings fixed about six feet from the ground were screwed into the pillars of the verandah, before every door, to fasten horses to, exactly as they are in an old Spanish town.

Against the wall of almost every house, just by the door, was set a chair or two of heavy wood, with the seat formed by strips of hide, on which the hair had formerly been left, but long ago rubbed off by use, or eaten by the ants.

The owner of the house sat with the back of the strong chair tilted against the wall, dressed in a loose and pleated shirt, with a high turned-down collar open at the throat, and spotless white duck trousers, that looked the whiter by their contrast with his brown, naked feet.

His home-made palm-tree hat was placed upon the ground beside him, and his cloak of coarse red baize was thrown back from his shoulders, as he sat smoking a cigarette rolled in a maize leaf, for in the Jesuit capillas only women smoked cigars.

At every angle of the square a sandy trail led out, either to the river or the woods, the little patches planted with mandioca, or to the maze of paths that, like the points outside a junction, eventually joined in one main trail, that ran from Itapua on the Paraná, up to Asuncion.

The church, built of wood cut in the neighbouring forest, had two tall towers, and followed in its plan the pattern of all the churches in the New World built by the Jesuits, from California down to the smallest mission in the south. It filled the fourth side of the square, and on each side of it there rose two feathery palms, known as the tallest in the Missions, which served as landmarks for travellers coming to the place, if they had missed their road. So large and well-proportioned was the church, it seemed impossible that it had been constructed solely by the Indians themselves, under the direction of the missionaries.

The overhanging porch and flight of steps that ran down to the grassy sward in the middle of the town gave it an air as of a cathedral reared to nature in the wilds, for the thick jungle flowed up behind it and almost touched its walls.

Bells of great size, either cast upon the spot or brought at vast expense from Spain, hung in the towers. On this, the feast day of the Blessed Virgin, the special patron of the settlement, they jangled ceaselessly, the Indians taking turns to haul upon the dried lianas that served instead of ropes. Though they pulled vigorously, the bells sounded a little muffled, as if they strove in vain against the vigorous nature that rendered any work of man puny and insignificant in the Paraguayan wilds.

Inside, the fane was dark, the images of saints were dusty, their paint was cracked, their gilding tarnished, making them look a little like the figures in a New Zealand pah, as they loomed through the darkness of the aisle. On the neglected altar, for at that time priests were a rarity in the Reductions, the Indians had placed great bunches of red flowers, and now and then a humming-bird flitted in through the glassless windows and hung poised above them; then darted out again, with a soft, whirring sound. Over the whole capilla, in which at one time several thousand Indians had lived, but now reduced to seventy or eighty at the most, there hung an air of desolation. It seemed as if man, in his long protracted struggle with the forces of the woods, had been defeated, and had accepted his defeat, content to vegetate, forgotten by the world, in the vast sea of green.

On this particular day, the annual festival of the Blessed Virgin, there was an air of animation, for from far and near, from Jesuit capilla, from straw-thatched huts lost in the clearings of the primeval forest, from the few cattle ranches that then existed, and from the little town of Itapua, fifty miles away, the scanty population had turned out to attend the festival.

Upon the forest tracks, from earliest dawn, long lines of white-clad women, barefooted, with their black hair cut square across the forehead and hanging down their backs, had marched as silently as ghosts. All of them smoked great, green cigars, and as they marched along, their leader carrying a torch, till the sun rose and jaguars went back to their lairs, they never talked; but if a woman in the rear of the long line wished to converse with any comrade in the front she trotted forward till she reached her friend and whispered in her ear. When they arrived at the crossing of the little river they bathed, or, at the least, washed carefully, and gathering a bunch of flowers, stuck them into their hair. They crossed the stream, and on arriving at the plaza they set the baskets, which they had carried on their heads, upon the ground, and sitting down beside them on the grass, spread out their merchandise. Oranges and bread, called "chipa," made from mandioca flour and cheese, with vegetables and various homely sweetmeats, ground nuts, rolls of sugar done up in plaintain leaves, and known as "rapadura," were the chief staples of their trade. Those who had asses let them loose to feed; and if upon the forest trails the women had been silent, once in the safety of the town no flight of parrots in a maize field could have chattered louder than they did as

they sat waiting by their wares. Soon the square filled, and men arriving tied their horses in the shade, slackening their broad hide girths, and piling up before them heaps of the leaves of the palm called "Pindó" in Guarani, till they were cool enough to eat their corn. Bands of boys, for in those days most of the men had been killed off in the past war, came trooping in, accompanied by crowds of women and of girls, who carried all their belongings, for there were thirteen women to a man, and the youngest boy was at a premium amongst the Indian women, who in the villages, where hardly any men were left, fought for male stragglers like unchained tigresses. A few old men came riding in on some of the few native horses left, for almost all the active, little, undersized breed of Paraguay had been exhausted in the war. They, too, had bands of women trotting by their sides, all of them anxious to unsaddle, to take the horses down to bathe, or to perform any small office that the men required of them. All of them smoked continuously, and each of them was ready with a fresh cigarette as soon as the old man or boy whom they accompanied finished the stump he held between his lips. The women all were dressed in the long Indian shirt called a "tupoi," cut rather low upon the breast, and edged with coarse black cotton lace, which every Paraguayan woman wore. Their hair was as black as a crow's back, and quite as shiny, and their white teeth so strong that they could tear the ears of corn out of a maize cob like a horse munching at his corn.

Then a few Correntino gauchos next appeared, dressed in their national costume of loose black merino trousers, stuffed into long boots, whose fronts were all embroidered in red silk. Their silver spurs, whose rowels were as large as saucers, just dangled off their heels, only retained in place by a flat chain, that met upon the instep, clasped with a lion's head. Long hair and brown vicuña ponchos, soft black felt hats, and red silk handkerchiefs tied loosely round their necks marked them as strangers, though they spoke Guarani.

They sat upon their silver-mounted saddles, with their toes resting in their bell-shaped stirrups, swaying so easily with every movement that the word riding somehow or other seemed inapplicable to men who, like the centaurs, formed one body with the horse.

As they drew near the plaza they raised their hands and touched their horses with the spur, and, rushing like a whirlwind right to the middle of the square, drew up so suddenly that their horses seemed to have turned to statues for a moment, and then at a slow trot, that made their silver trappings jingle as they went, slowly rode off into the shade.

The plaza filled up imperceptibly, and the short grass was covered by a white-clad throng of Indians. The heat increased, and all the time the bells rang out, pulled vigorously by relays of Indians, and at a given signal the people turned and trooped towards the church, all carrying flowers in their hands.

As there was no one to sing Mass, and as the organ long had been neglected, the congregation listened to some prayers, read from a book of Hours by an old Indian, who pronounced the Latin, of which most likely he did not understand a word, as if it had been Guarani. They sang "Las Flores á Maria" all in unison, but keeping such good time that at a little distance from the church it sounded like waves breaking on a beach after a summer storm.

In the neglected church, where no priest ministered or clergy prayed, where all the stoops of holy water had for years been dry, and where the Mass had been well-nigh forgotten as a whole, the spirit lingered, and if it quickeneth upon that feast day in the Paraguayan missions, that simple congregation were as uplifted by it as if the sacrifice had duly been fulfilled with candles, incense, and the pomp and ceremony of Holy Mother Church upon the Seven Hills.

As every one except the Correntinos went barefooted, the exit of the congregation made no noise except the sound of naked feet, slapping a little on the wooden steps, and so the people silently once again filled the plaza, where a high wooden arch had been erected in the middle, for the sport of running at the ring.

The vegetable sellers had now removed from the middle of the square, taking all their wares under the long verandah, and several pedlars had set up their booths and retailed cheap European trifles such as no one in the world but a Paraguayan Indian could possibly require. Razors that would not cut, and little looking-glasses in pewter frames made in Thuringia, cheap clocks that human ingenuity was powerless to repair when they had run their course of six months' intermittent ticking, and gaudy pictures representing saints who had ascended to the empyrean, as it appeared, with the clothes that they had worn in life, and all bald-headed, as befits a saint, were set out side by side with handkerchiefs of the best China silk. Sales were concluded after long-continued chaffering – that higgling of the market dear to old-time economists, for no one would have bought the smallest article, even below cost price, had it been offered to him at the price the seller originally asked.

Enrique Clerici, from Itapua, had transported all his pulperia bodily for the occasion of the feast. It had not wanted more than a small wagon to contain his stock-in-trade. Two or three dozen bottles of square-faced gin of the Anchor brand, a dozen of heady red wine from Catalonia, a pile of sardine boxes, sweet biscuits, raisins from Malaga, esparto baskets full of figs, and sundry pecks of apricots dried in the sun and cut into the shape of ears, and hence called "orejones," completed all his store. He himself, tall and sunburnt, stood dressed in riding-boots and a broad hat, with his revolver in his belt, beside a pile of empty bottles, which he had always ready, to hurl at customers if there should be any attempt either at cheating or to rush his wares. He spoke the curious lingo, half-Spanish, half-Italian, that so many of his countrymen use in the River Plate; and all his conversation ran upon Garibaldi, with whom he had campaigned in youth, upon Italia Irredenta, and on the time when anarchy should sanctify mankind by blood, as he said, and bring about the reign of universal brotherhood.

He did a roaring trade, despite the competition of a native Paraguayan, who had brought three demi-johns of Caña, for men prefer the imported article the whole world over, though it is vile, to native manufactures, even when cheap and good.

Just about twelve o'clock, when the sun almost burned a hole into one's head, the band got ready in the church porch, playing upon old instruments, some of which may have survived from Jesuit times, or, at the least, been copied in the place, as the originals decayed.

Sackbuts and psalteries and shawms were there, with serpents, gigantic clarionets, and curiously twisted oboes, and drums, whose canvas all hung slack and gave a muffled sound when they were beaten, and little fifes, ear-piercing and devilish, were represented in that band. It banged and crashed "La Palomita," that tune of evil-sounding omen, for to its strains prisoners were always ushered out to execution in the times of Lopez, and as it played the players slowly walked down the steps.

Behind them followed the alcalde, an aged Indian, dressed in long cotton drawers, that at the knees were split into a fringe that hung down to his ankles, a spotless shirt much pleated, and a red cloak of fine merino cloth. In his right hand he carried a long cane with a silver head – his badge of office. Walking up to the door of his own house, by which was set a table covered with glasses and with home-made cakes, he gave the signal for the running at the ring.

The Correntino gauchos, two or three Paraguayans, and a German married to a Paraguayan wife, were all who entered for the sport. The band struck up, and a young Paraguayan started the first course. Gripping his stirrups tightly between his naked toes, and seated on an old "recao," surmounted by a sheepskin, he spurred his horse, a wall-eyed skewbald, with his great iron spurs, tied to his bare insteps with thin strips of hide. The skewbald, only half-tamed, reared once or twice and bounded off, switching its ragged tail, which had been half-eaten off by cows. The people yelled, a "mosqueador!" – that is, a "fly-flapper," a grave fault in a horse in the eyes of Spanish Americans – as the Paraguayan steered the skewbald with the reins held high in his left hand, carrying the other just above the level of his eyes, armed with a piece of cane about a foot in length.

As he approached the arch, in which the ring dangled from a string, his horse, either frightened by the shouting of the crowd or by the arch itself, swerved and plunged violently, carrying its rider through the thickest of the people, who separated like a flock of sheep when a dog runs through it, cursing him volubly. The German came the next, dressed in his Sunday clothes, a slop-made suit of shoddy cloth, riding a horse that all his spurring could not get into full speed. The rider's round, fair face was burned a brick-dust colour, and as he spurred and plied his whip, made out of solid tapir hide, the sweat ran down in streams upon his coat. So intent was he on flogging, that as he neared the ring he dropped his piece of cane, and his horse, stopping suddenly just underneath the arch, would have unseated him had he not clasped it round the neck. Shouts of delight greeted this feat of horsemanship, and one tall Correntino, taking his cigarette out of his mouth, said to his fellow sitting next to him upon his horse, "The very animals themselves despise the gringos. See how that little white-nosed brute that he was riding knew that he was a 'maturango,' and nearly had him off."

Next came Hijinio Rojas, a Paraguayan of the better classes, sallow and Indian looking, dressed in clothes bought in Asuncion, his trousers tucked into his riding-boots. His small black hat, with the brim flattened up against his head by the wind caused by the fury of the gallop of his active little roan with four white feet, was kept upon his head by a black ribbon knotted underneath his chin. As he neared the arch his horse stepped double several times and fly-jumped; but that did not disturb him in the least, and, aiming well he touched the ring, making it fly into the air. A shout went up, partly in Spanish, partly in Guarani, from the assembled people, and Rojas, reining in his horse, stopped him in a few bounds, so sharply, that his unshod feet cut up the turf of the green plaza as a skate cuts the ice. He turned and trotted gently to the arch, and then, putting his horse to its top speed, stopped it again beside the other riders, amid the "Vivas" of the crowd. Then came the turn of the four Correntinos, who rode good horses from their native province, had silver horse-gear and huge silver spurs, that dangled from their heels. They were all gauchos, born, as the saying goes, "amongst the animals." A dun with fiery eyes and a black stripe right down his back, and with black markings on both hocks, a chestnut skewbald, a "doradillo," and a horse of that strange mealy bay with a fern-coloured muzzle, that the gauchos call a "Pangaré," carried them just as if their will and that of those who rode them were identical. Without a signal, visible at least to any but themselves, their horses started at full speed, reaching occasionally at the bit, then dropping it again and bridling so easy that one could ride them with a thread drawn from a spider's web. Their riders sat up easily, not riding as a European rides, with his eyes fixed upon each movement of his horse, but, as it were, divining them as soon as they were made. Each of them took the ring, and all of them checked their horses, as it were, by their volition, rather than the bit, making the silver horse-gear rattle and their great silver spurs jingle upon their feet. Each waited for the other at the far side of the arch, and then turning in a line they started with a shout, and as they passed right through the middle of the square at a wild gallop, they swung down sideways from their saddles and dragged their hands upon the ground. Swinging up, apparently without an effort, back into their seats, when they arrived at the point from where they had first started, they reined up suddenly, making their horses plunge and rear, and then by a light signal on the reins stand quietly in line, tossing the foam into the air. Hijinio Rojas and the four centaurs all received a prize, and the alcalde, pouring out wineglasses full of gin, handed them to the riders, who, with a compliment or two as to the order of their drinking, emptied them solemnly.

No other runners having come forward to compete, for in those days horses were scarce throughout the Paraguayan Missions, the sports were over, and the perspiring crowd went off to breakfast at tables spread under the long verandahs, and silence fell upon the square.

The long, hot hours during the middle of the day were passed in sleeping. Some lay face downwards in the shade. Others swung in white cotton hammocks, keeping them in perpetual motion, till they fell asleep, by pushing with a naked toe upon the ground. At last the sun, the enemy, as the Arabs call him, slowly declined, and white-robed women, with their "tupois" slipping half off their necks, began to come out into the verandahs, slack and perspiring after the midday struggle with the heat.

Then bands of girls sauntered down to the river, from whence soon came the sound of merry laughter as they splashed about and bathed.

The Correntinos rode down to a pool and washed their horses, throwing the water on them with their two hands, as the animals stood nervously shrinking from each splash, until they were quite wet through and running down, when they stood quietly, with their tails tucked in between their legs.

Night came on, as it does in those latitudes, no twilight intervening, and from the rows of houses came the faint lights of wicks burning in bowls of grease, whilst from beneath the orange trees was heard the tinkling of guitars.

Enormous bats soared about noiselessly, and white-dressed couples lingered about the corners of the streets, and men stood talking, pressed closely up against the wooden gratings of the windows, to women hidden inside the room. The air was heavy with the languorous murmur of the tropic night, and gradually the lights one by one were extinguished, and the tinkling of the guitars was stilled. The moon came out, serene and glorious, showing each stone upon the sandy trails as clearly as at midday. Saddling their horses, the four Correntinos silently struck the trail to Itapua, and bands of women moved off along the forest tracks towards their homes, walking in Indian file. Hijinio Rojas, who had saddled up to put the Correntinos on the right road, emerged into the moonlit plaza, his shadow outlined so sharply on the grass it seemed it had been drawn, and then, entering a side street, disappeared into the night. The shrill neighing of his horse appeared as if it bade farewell to its companions, now far away upon the Itapua trail. Noises that rise at night from forests in the tropics sound mysteriously, deep in the woods. It seemed as if a population silent by day was active and on foot, and from the underwood a thick white mist arose, shrouding the sleeping town.

Little by little, just as a rising tide covers a reef of rocks, it submerged everything in its white, clinging folds. The houses disappeared, leaving the plaza seething like a lake, and then the church was swallowed up, the towers struggling, as it were, a little, just as a wreath of seaweed on a rock appears to fight against the tide. Then they too disappeared, and the conquering mist enveloped everything. All that was left above the sea of billowing white were the two topmost tufts of the tall, feathery palms.

EL RODEO

The vast, brown, open space, sometimes a quarter of a mile across, called El Rodeo, which bears the same relation to the ocean of tall grass that a shoal bears to the surface of the sea, was the centre of the life of the great cattle *estancias* of the plains. To it on almost every morning of the year the cattle were collected and taught to stand there till the dew was off the grass. To *parar rodeo* was the phrase the Gauchos used, equivalent to the cowboys' "round up" on the northern plains.

An hour before the dawn, when the moon was down, but the sun not up, just at the time when the first streaks of red begin to fleck the sky, the Gauchos had got up from their *recaos*. In those days it was a point of honour to sleep on the *recao*, the *carona* spread out on the ground, the *jergas* on it, the *cojinillo* underneath the hips for softness, the head pillowed upon *los bastos*, and under them your pistol, knife, your *tirador*, and boots, yourself wrapped up in your *poncho* and with your head tied up in a handkerchief. The Gauchos had looked out in the frost or dew, according to the season of the year, to see the horse they had tied up overnight had not got twisted in his stake-rope, and then returned to sit before the fire to take a *matecito cimarron* and smoke. Every now and then a man had left the fire, and,

lifting the dried mare's-hide that served for door, had come back
silently, and, sitting down again, taken a bit of burning wood, ladling
it from the fire, upon his knife's edge, and lit his cigarette. At last,
when the coming dawn had lit the sky like an Aurora Borealis lights a
northern winter's night, they had risen silently, and shouldering
their saddles, had gone out silently to saddle up.

Outside the horses stood and shivered on their ropes, their backs
arched up like cats about to fight. Frequently when their intending
rider had drawn the pin to which they were attached, and after coiling
up the rope approached them warily, they sat back snorting like a
steam-engine when it breasts a hill. If it was possible, the Gaucho
saddled his horse after first hobbling his front feet, although he was
sure to throw the saddle-cloths and the *carona* several times upon
the ground. When they were put firmly upon his back, the rider,
cautiously stretching his naked foot under the horse's belly, caught
up the cinch between his toes. Passing the *latigo* between the strong
iron rings, both of the *encimera* and the cinch, he put his foot against
the horse's side and pulled till it was like an hour-glass, which
operation not infrequently set the horse bucking, hobbled as he was.

If, on the other hand, the horse was but half-tamed, a *redomon* as
the phrase was, his owner led him up to the *palenque*, tied him up
firmly to it, and after hobbling and perhaps blindfolding him saddled
him, after a fierce struggle and an accompaniment of snorts. When all
was ready, and the first light was just about to break, showing the
Pampa silvery with mist and dew, and in the winter morning often
presenting curious mirages of woods hung in the sky, the trees suspen-
ded upside down, the *capataz* would give the signal to set off. Going
up gently to their horses, the Gauchos carefully untied them, taking
good care no coil of the *maneador* should get caught in their feet, and
then after tightening the broad hide girth, often eight or nine inches
broad, led them a little forward to let them get their backs down, or
buck if they so felt inclined. Then they all mounted, some of the horses
whirling round at a gallop, their riders holding their heads towards
them by the *bozal* in the left hand, and with the reins and pommel of
the saddle in the right. They mounted in a way peculiar to themselves,
bending the knee and passing it over the middle of the saddle, but never
dwelling on the stirrup, after the European way, so that the action
seemed one motion, and they were on their horses as easily as a drop of
water runs down a window-pane, and quite as noiselessly.

Calling the dogs, generally a troop of mongrels of all sorts, with perhaps a thin black greyhound or two amongst the pack, the Gauchos used to ride off silently, their horses leaving a trail of footsteps in the dew. Some bucked and plunged, their riders shouting as their long hair and *ponchos* flapped up and down at every bound the horses made. They left the *estancia* always at the *trotecito*, the horses putting up their backs, arching their necks and playing with the bit, whose inside rollers, known as *coscojo*, jingled on their teeth.

Then after a hundred yards or so one would look at the others and say "Vamos," the rest would answer "Vamonos" and set off galloping, until the *capataz* would order them to separate, telling them such and such a "point" of cattle should be about the hill which is above the river of the *sarandis*, there is a bald-faced cow in it, curly all over; you cannot miss her if you try. Other "points" would have a bullock with a broken horn in them, or some other animal, impossible to miss . . . to eyes trained to the plains.

In a moment all the horsemen disappeared into the "camp" just as the first rays of the sun came out to melt the dew upon the grass. This was called *campeando*, and the owner or the *capataz* usually made his aim some "point" of cattle which was the tamest and fed closest to the house, and probably contained all the tame oxen and a milk cow or two. When he had found them he drove them slowly to the *rodeo*, which they approached all bellowing, the younger animals striking into a run before they reached it, and all of them halting when they felt their feet on the bare ground. Once there, the *capataz*, lighting a cigarette, walked his horse slowly to and fro, occasionally turning back any animal that tried to separate and go back to the grass.

Most likely he would wait an hour, or perhaps two, during which time the sun ascending gathered strength and brought out a keen, acrid smell from the hard-trodden earth of the *rodeo*, on which for years thousands of cattle had been driven up each day. The "point" of cattle already there would soon begin to hang their heads and stand quite motionless, the *capataz* horse either become impatient or go off into a contemplative state, resting alternately one each hind leg.

Such of the dogs who had remained with him would stretch themselves at full length on the grass. At last faint shouts and sounds of galloping and baying dogs would be heard in the distance, gradually drawing near.

Then a dull thundering of countless feet, and by degrees, from north,

south, east and west, would come great "points" of cattle galloping. Behind, waving their *ponchos*, brandishing their short *rebenques* round their heads, raced the *vaqueros*, followed by the dogs. As each "point" reached the *rodeo* the galloping men would check their foaming horses so that the cattle might arrive at a slow pace and not cause a stampede amongst the animals that were already on the spot.

At last all the "points" had arrived. Three, four, five or ten thousand cattle were assembled, and the men who had brought them from the thick cane-brakes and from the *montes* of the deltas of the streams, after having loosed their girths and lit cigarettes, proceeded slowly to ride round the herd to keep them on the spot. The dogs lay panting with their tongues lolling out of their mouths, the sun began to bite a little, and now and then a wild bullock or light-footed young cow, or even a small "point" of cattle, would break away, to try to get back to its *querencia* or merely out of fright.

Then with a shout a horseman, starting with a bound, his horse all fire, his own long hair streaming out in the wind, would dart out after them, to try to head them back. "Vuelta ternero," "Vuelta vaquilla" they would cry, riding a little wide of the escaping beast. After a hundred yards or so, for the first rush of the wild native cattle was swift as lightning, the rider would close in. Riding in front of the escaping truant, he would try to turn it back, pressing his horse against its side.

If it turned, as was generally the case, towards the herd, after three or four hundred yards of chase, the Gaucho checked his horse and let the animal return at a slow gallop by itself till it had joined the rest.

If it was a fierce bullock or a fleet-footed cow, and even after he had bored it to one side it started out again, or stopped and charged, he rode beside it beating it with the handle of his *arreador*. When all these means had failed, as a last resource he sometimes ran his horse's chest against its flank, and gave it thus a heavy fall. This was called giving a *pechada* and if repeated a few times usually cowed the wildest of the herd, though now and then an escaping animal had to be lassoed and dragged back and then if it broke out again the Gauchos used to rope it, and after throwing it, dissect a bit of skin between the eyes, so that it fell and blinded the poor beast and stopped him running off. These were the humours of the scene, till after half an hour or so of gently riding round and round, the *rodeo*, from having been at first a bellowing, kaleidoscopic mass of horns and hoofs, of flashing eyes and tails lashing about, like snakes, a mere confusion of all colours, black, white and brown, dun, cream and red, in an inextricable maze, became distinguishable, and you perceived the various "points," each recognizable by some outstanding beast, either in colour or in shape. The *capataz* and all the Gauchos knew them, just as a sailor knows all kinds of ships, and in an instant, with a quick look, could tell if such and such a beast was fat, or only in the state known to the adept as *carne blanca*, or if the general condition of the herd was good, and this with a *rodeo* of five thousand animals.

Their searching eyes detected at a glance if a beast had received a wound of any kind, if maggots had got into the sore and sometimes on the spot the cow or bullock thus affected would be lassoed, cast, its wound washed out with salt and water, and then allowed to rise. Needless to say, this operation did not improve its temper, and as occasionally, in order to save trouble, the Gauchos did not rope it by the neck and put another rope on the hind legs, both horses straining on the ropes to keep them taut, but merely roped and cast and then put a fore leg above the horn, and let a man hold down the beast by pulling on its tail passed under the hind leg, the man who stood, holding the cow's horn full of the "remedy," was left in a tight place.

If he had not an easy horse to mount, the infuriated beast sometimes pursued him with such quickness that he had to dive beneath the belly and mount from the offside. If by an evil chance his horse broke away from him to avoid the charge, two Gauchos rushing like the wind, their iron handled whips raised in the air like flails, ready to fall upon the bullock's back, closed in upon the beast and fenced him in between their horses, at full speed and as they passed, thundering upon the plain, men, horses and the flying animal all touching one another and straining every nerve, the man in peril, seizing the instant that they passed, sprang lightly up behind the near-side rider, just as a head of thistledown stops for a moment on the edge of a tall bank, tops it, and disappears.

When the *rodeo* had stood an hour or so, if nothing else was in the wind, the *vaqueros*, galloped home slowly, smoking and talking of the price of cattle in the *saladeros*, the races to be held next Sunday at some *pulperia* or other, "La Flor de Mayo," "La Rosa del Sur," or "La Esquina de los pobres Diablos" and the *rodeo*, when it felt itself alone, slowly disintegrated just as a crowd breaks up after a meeting in Hyde Park and all the various "points" sought out their grazing grounds.

On days when they required fresh meat at the *estancia*, when it was necessary in Gaucho phrase to *carnear*, then the *capataz* and two *peenes*, coiling their *lazos* as they went, rode into the *rodeo*, the cattle parting into lanes before them, and after much deliberation and pointing here and there, with sage remarks on the condition of the herd, he would point his finger at a beast. Then, cautiously, the two *vaqueros*, with the loop of their *lazo* trailing on the ground, taking good care to hold it in their right hands, high and wide, so that their horses did not tread in it, would close upon their prey. Watching him carefully, the horses turning almost before the men gave them the signal with the hand or heel, the cattle edging away from them, they would conduct the animal towards the edge of the *rodeo* with his head to the "camp."

When he was clear, with a shrill cry they spurred their horses and the doomed beast began to gallop, unless perchance he doubled back towards the herd, in which contingency the operation had to be gone through again. Once galloping, the efforts of the riders were directed to keep him on the move, which in proportion to his wildness was harder or more easy to achieve, for a wild cow or bullock generally "parts" more easily than a tame animal. Perhaps the distance was a mile, and this they traversed at full gallop, hair, *poncho*, mane, and tail all flying in the wind, with a thin cloud of dust marking their passage as they went. When they got near the house one rider looked up at the other and said, "Now is the time to throw." In an instant, round his head revolved the thin hide-plaited rope, the ring (the last six feet in double plait) shining and glistening in the sun. The wrist turned like a well-oiled machine, the horse sprang forward with a bound, and the rope, winding like a snake, whistled and hurtled through the air.

It fixed as if by magic round the horns, the rider generally keeping in his hand some coils of slack for any casuality that might occur. The instant that it settled round the horns the rider spurred his horse away to the left side, for it was death to get entangled in the rope. In fact, in every cattle district maimed hands and feet showed plainly how dangerous was the game. The check called the *tirón* came when the animal had galloped twenty yards or so. It brought him to a stop, his hind legs sliding to one side. The horse leaned over, straining on the rope, the victim bellowed and rolled its eyes, lashing its tail against its flanks and pawing up the turf.

If the position of the animal was near enough, so as to save the carriage of the meat, the last act straight began. If not, after avoiding dexterously a charge or two, keeping the rope taut, and free from his horse's legs or even sides or croup, unless he was a well-trained cattle horse, the other *peon* riding up behind, twisting his *lazo* round his head, urging his horse against the lassoed animal, rode up and drove him nearer in. Once within handy distance from the house, the man who had been driving threw his rope and caught the bullock by the heels. Sometimes they threw him down and butchered him; at other times, the man who had him by the horns, keeping his *lazo* taut, he and his horse throwing their weight upon the rope, called to his fellow to dismount and *carnear*.

If he was an expert, throwing his reins upon the ground, he slipped off quickly, and crouching like a jaguar about to spring, ran cautiously to the offside of the enlassoed beast, drawing his long *facón*. Avoiding any desperate horn-thrust, like a cat avoids a stone, and taking care not to get mixed up with the rope, he plunged his knife deep down into the throat. The gushing stream of blood sprang like the water from a fire-plug, and the doomed creature sank upon its knees, then rocked a little to and fro, and with a bellow of distress, fell and expired.

If, on the other hand, the animal was fierce, or the man did not care to run the risk, he advanced, and, drawing his *facón* across its hocks, hamstrung it, and brought it to the ground, and then came up and killed it when it was rendered helpless. On such occasions it was terrible and quite enough to set a man against all beef for ever (had there been any other food upon the plains) to see the bullock jumping upon its mutilated legs and hear it bellow in its agony.

Last scene of all, the horses either unsaddled or attached to the *palenque*, or else to a stout post of the corral, the slayers taking off their *ponchos* or their coats, skinned and cut up the beast. So rapidly was this achieved, that sometimes hardly an hour had elapsed from the "death bellow," to the time when the raw joints of meat were hung in the *galpón*. The hide was stretched out in the sun, and the *chumangos* and the dogs feasted upon the entrails, whilst the wild riders, dusty and bloodstained, took a *maté* in the shade.

There was another and a wilder aspect of the *rodeo*, which, like a *pampero*, burst on the beholders so suddenly that when it passed and all had settled down again, they gazed, half stunned, out on the tranquil plain. It might be that a *tropero* was parting cattle for a *saladero*, his men cutting out cattle, riding them towards a "point" of working bullocks, held back by men about a quarter of a mile from the main body of the herd. All might be going well, the *rodeo* kept back by men riding round slowly. The parties might be working quietly, without much shouting; the day serene, the sun unclouded, when suddenly an uneasy movement would run through the cattle, making them sway and move about, after the fashion of the water in a whirlpool, without apparent cause.

If the *tropero* and the overseer or the owner of the place himself were men who knew the "camp," and few of them were ignorant of all its lore, they did not lose a moment, but calling as gently as possible to the *peones*, they made them ride as close to one another as they could, in a great circle round about the beasts. It might be that their efforts would pacify the animals, but in all cases the "cutting out" was over for the day.

A little thing, a hat blown off, a *poncho* waving, a horse suddenly starting or falling in a hole, would render all their efforts useless and as vain as those of him who seeks to keep a flight of locusts from lighting on a field. In an instant the cattle would go mad, their eyes flash fire, their tails and heads go up, and, with a surge, the whole *rodeo*, perhaps five or six thousand beasts would, with a universal bellow, and a noise as of a mighty river in full flood, break into a stampede. Nothing could stay their passage, over hills, down steep *quebradas*, and through streams they dashed, just as a prairie fire flies through the grass. Then was the time to see the Gaucho at his best, his hat blown back, held by a broad black ribbon underneath his chin, and as he flew along, slipping his *poncho* off the *capataz* galloped to head the torrent of mad beasts.

The *peones*, spreading out like the sticks of a fan, urged on their horses with their great iron spurs, and with resounding blows of their *rebenques* as they strove hard to close and get in front. Those who were caught amongst the raging mass held their lives only by their horses' feet, pushed here and there against the animals, but still unmoved, upright and watchful in their saddles, and quick to seize the slightest opportunity of making their way out. If by mischance their horses fell, their fate was sealed; and the tornado past, their bodies lay upon the plain, like those of sailors washed ashore after a shipwreck – distorted, horrible.

The men who at the first had spread out on the sides, now closing in, had got in front, and galloped at the head of the mad torrent, waving their *ponchos* and brandishing their whips. They, too, were in great peril of their lives if the herd crossed a viscachera or a *cangrejal*. That was the time for prodigies of horsemanship. If I but close my eyes, I see, at a stampede on an *estancia* called "El Calá," a semi-Indian rushing down a slope to head the cattle off. His horse was a dark dun, with eyes of fire, a black stripe down the middle of his back, and curious black markings on the hocks. His tail floated out in the wind, and helped him in his turnings, just as a steering oar deflects a whaleboat's prow. The brand was a small "s" inside a shield. I saw it as they passed. Down the steep slope they thundered, the Indian's hair rising and falling at each spring that the black dun made in his course. His great iron spurs hung off his heels, and all his silver gear, the reins, the *pasadores* of the stirrups, the *chapeao* and *fiadór*, and the great spurs themselves, jingled and clinked as he tore on to head the living maelstrom of the stampeding beasts. Suddenly his horse, although sure-footed, keen, and practised at the work, stepped in a hole and turned a somersault.

He fell, just as a stone from the nippers of a crane, and his wild rider, opening his legs, lit on his feet so truly, that his great iron spurs clanked on the ground like fetters, as he stood holding the halter in his hand. As his horse bounded to his feet, his rider, throwing down his head and tucking his left elbow well into his side, sprang at a bound upon his back and galloped on, so rapidly that it appeared I had been dreaming, and only have woke up, thirty years after, to make sure of my dream. Sometimes the efforts of the *peones* were successful and the first panic stayed, the cattle let themselves be broken into "points," and by degrees and with great management were driven back to the *rodeo* and kept there for an hour or two till they had quieted down. If, on the other hand, they kept on running, they ran for leagues, till they encountered a river or a lake and, plunging into it, many were drowned, and in all cases many were sure to stray and mix with other herds, or, wandering away, never returned again.

The whole impression of the scene was unforgettable, and through the dust, both of the prairie and the thicker dust of years, I can see still the surging of the living lava stream, and hear its thunder on the plain.

THE BOLAS

"They have certain balls of stone" (says Hulderico Schmidel in his "Historia y Descubrimiento del Rio de la Plata y Paraguay") "tied to a long string like to our chain shot; they throw them at the legs of the horses (or of the deer when they hunt), which brings them to the ground, and with these bolas they killed our Captain and the above referred to gentlemen."

This happened in the year 1585, when the Flemish soldier Hulderico Schmidel fought with the troops of Pedro de Mendoza against the Indians called Querandis, on what is now the site of Buenos Ayres. The captain slain was Diego de Mendoza, brother to the general of the expedition; the "above referred to gentlemen" figure but as "los seis Hidalgos." And thus is chronicled the first description of the "bolas," destined since then to bring down to the ground many a good horse and stag, and even crush the skulls of captains and hidalgos not a few.

Confined entirely to the south of South America, the bolas, like the boomerang, seems to have been unknown to any tribe of savages apart from its inventors. It grew, like other national weapons, from the conditions of the life and country whence it sprang.

The Indians of South America before the Conquest had no horses, so, living on great plains, game must have been most difficult to approach, and when approached consisted chiefly of deer, guanacos, and of ostriches – all animals certain to escape (upon a plain) if slightly wounded by an arrow. Thus an invention like the bolas, which if it touched the legs was certain to entangle, was valuable, as, thrown by a strong arm, it could be used almost as far off as an arrow, was much more easily recovered after a miss, and ten times easier to make. Schmidel describes the weapon accurately when he refers to it as "three balls of stone fastened together by a cord after the fashion of our chain shot." Therefore, it will be seen that the bolas known (for euphony and other reasons) as "las boleadores" in the River Plate stands in the same relation to the lazo as the rifle stands to the ordinary gun.

Such as it is, no Indian, Gaucho, or any self-respecting countryman from Sandy Point to Paraguay, or from the Banda Oriental to Coronel, ever stirs out without at least one pair, either wound round his waist or placed under the "cojinillo" of his saddle, ready to throw at ostriches, at deer, guanacos, or at the horse of some newcomer to the country which has escaped and scours the plain, the stirrups dangling to the accompaniment of shouts of "Yá se vá el caballo del Inglés." Sometimes it serves to fight with at a "pulpería," when the inevitable gin-born discussion as to the merits of the "Blancos" and the "Colorados" waxes hot.

Bolas for general use are made of two stones about the size and weight of billiard balls, and of another about half the size and egg-shaped. All three are shrunk into bags of hide known to the Gaucho as "retobas." Each ball is fastened to a string of twisted hide about the thickness of a pencil, and three feet in length. The three are fastened in the middle like a Manxman's legs, so that the length from the hand ball to the two large balls does not exceed six feet, and the whole weight is not above a pound. For horses, wooden balls are used, and to catch ostriches, little balls of lead not larger than a pigeon's egg, fastened to strings of rather greater length than those I have described.

The Indians in the south of Patagonia sometimes use a bola made of a single string and with a ball attached, with which they strike and kill wild animals, as pumas, jaguars, and guanacos. The instrument is called "bola perdida," and, of course, cannot be used to take an animal alive, as it does not entangle but merely stuns the animal it strikes. At other times they use a single string with but a single bola and a hand ball, as being easier to throw, lighter to carry, and much easier to make, but it does not wind round the legs so firmly as do the bolas of the common shape. To throw the bolas, they are whirled round the head and circle through the air with the two heavier balls close beside one another, and when launched turn round and round on their own axis in their flight, and break in like a "twister" from the leg side, and if the strings strike on the legs of any animal, the motion of the bolas being stopped, the balls wind round and round and tie the animal as firmly as would a pair of hobbles. The heavier kind may (on a good horse) be thrown from fifty to seventy yards, the balls for ostriches nearly one hundred, and the single "bola perdida" a hundred and twenty yards and even more, according to the strength of the man throwing and the speed at which the cast is made. On foot, as with the lazo, much of the power is lost, though as a general rule the cast is made more accurately. When thrown the bolas are extremely hard to get away from, and the best plan is to run towards the thrower and lie down flat upon the ground. If the man thrown at tries to run away his chance is small, and even if armed with a revolver the odds are much in favour of the "boleador," especially if he has several pairs of bolas, as, at the distance of fifty to sixty yards, the pistol rarely does damage if the object at which the shooter aims is moving rapidly about; the fact of motion is of no consequence to the man who throws the "balls," their length giving such a wide margin upon which to work. The bolas are easier by far to learn than is the lazo, and the danger far less great; for as the bolas leave the hand when thrown, the only danger lies in the possibility of catching your own horse's legs, in which case it is probable he will start bucking "fit to knock down a town," and the unlucky thrower get a violent fall and rise to find his horse either with a leg broken or else scouring the plain with his new saddle, and himself afoot.

An average horseman and a cricket-player should learn the bolas in three months' practice though to excel (as with the lazo) the "boleador" must have begun as a mere child, and have "balled" and "lazoed" chickens, cats, and dogs in order to acquire the skill of hand the natives of the Pampas enjoy with both. Such is the weapon (well greased with mutton fat) with which the Gaucho and the Indian fight, catch wild horses, deer, and ostriches, and with which their

forefathers caught the horses of the soldiers of Don Pedro de Mendoza, and their grandfathers the artillerymen of the unlucky expedition under General Whitelock, the flags of which still hang in Buenos Ayres in the Cathedral aisle.

In the vast territory of the Southern Pampa, which stretches from Bahia Blanca to Sandy Point, and from Puan to Nahuelhuapi; in the green prairies that reach from Buenos Ayres to the Sierra de Vulcan, upon the park-like prairies of Entre Rios, and the vast rolling steppes of Rio Grande, and again amongst the apple forests to the Andes, the bolas are the chief pleasure, weapon, and plaything of the Gaucho of the plains. His habits, speech, and mode of life Azara first made known to the futile world which reads and writes, and thinks because it reads it knows, and to whose eyes the Pampa with its signs, its lore, its disappearing customs, its low horizons, flat-topped ombús, rivers and wastes, Guadal and Biscacheras, its flocks of ostriches, its cattle without number, herds of wild horses, whirling tero-teros, and its lone ranches, is a closed book. Nothing so pleasant in this machine-rid world as to bestride a half-tamed horse upon the Southern Pampas, and, well armed with several pairs of ostrich bolas, accompanied by two good greyhounds, to go upon the "boleada" – that is, to start out ostrich hunting with several well-tried friends, and with a "caballada" from which to take a fresh mount when the horse ridden tires. The Patagonian ostrich (*Rhea Americana*) frequents the stony uplands which so fascinated Darwin, and of which he said that all the wealth of vegetation of the tropics had not made so deep a mark upon his mind as the wild plains, the solitary huts, the lonely camp-fires where the dogs kept watch, the horses eating, tied with their green-hide ropes, and he lay smoking, wrapped in his poncho, looking at the stars. Whether in Patagonia, or on the rolling plains of brown and waving grass which stretch from the Romero Grande to Tandil, the ostrich goes in flocks ranging from ten or twelve up to a hundred or even more. Scudding across the plains before the wind, their wings spread out to catch the breeze, it takes a well-tried horse, with his utmost efforts, after a gallop of several miles, to bring a man within a bola's cast. The hunters range themselves in a formation like a fan, and try to join the outside edges of their ranks and get the ostriches into a circle, or else to force them into marshy ground on which they cannot run, or up against the margin of a stream, edge of a wood, or border of a precipice. Sometimes the birds scatter and break up into groups, and then the horsemen, whirling their bolas round their heads, bound over stones, rush through the mia-mia, thread through the scrub, and, with wild cries, incite their horses and their greyhounds to full speed. Ponchos stream in the wind, hair flutters, silver spurs rattle upon the raw hide girths, and now and then a horse, stepping into a "cangrejal," rolls like a rabbit, its rider seldom failing to alight "parado" – that is, on his feet – and, holding the long reins or halter in his hand, to rise before his horse, and mounting, when it regains its legs, straight to resume the chase.

To go upon the "boleada" is the chief ambition of every Gaucho of the south, and so that he can make enough to keep him in cigars and gin, to buy a new silk handkerchief or poncho now and then, no chance that he will hire himself for any settled work. Yet many of the "boleadores" die at their trade, either at the hands of Indians, by hunger or by thirst, or, failing to alight "parado" after a heavy fall, are left on foot with a limb broken, to die alone amidst the ocean of brown grass, from which no man left wounded, without a horse, escapes alive. Most of the frontier soldiers who, in the last two generations, themselves half Indians, have forced the Indians back into the wild valleys of the Cordillera of the Andes, have been "boleadores."

The couriers, who used to ride from Bahia Blancas to Patagonia, passing the Rio Colorado, and getting across the "travesia" as best they might, all learned their desert lore in the pursuit of ostriches. Perhaps Bahia Blanca was the centre of the "bolas." Game was abundant, cattle mostly wild, Indians swept often in their "malones" over the settled lands, and the wild people known as "Badilleros" had a deep-rooted and most logical objection to all continued work. Even the lazo was too troublesome, and so they lived even less comfortably than did the Indians, raising no crops, shivering in wretched mud and straw-thatched huts, with a horse-hide for the door, eating no bread, and with a saddled horse tied night and day outside the house. Their conversation was all of horses, brands, fights with the Indians, feats with the "bolas"; of such a one who, on his journey to some place, was set on by the "infidel," and crossed the Rio Colorado with a pair of bolas on his horse's legs; of such another who, carrying the mails, lost the road, and was discovered lying dead on his exhausted horse, his last act having been to hang the mailbag on a tree.

Such as they were, a hardy race – now passed, or passing fast, into oblivion – more savage than the Arabs, only a step advanced beyond the Indians; tall, lean, long-haired, hospitable, and thievish, abstemious as Icelanders, and yet as very gluttons as an Apache at a dog feast; born almost on their horses, sitting them like centaurs, living amongst them, talking and thinking but of them, and shying when they shied, as they had been one flesh. I see them, as I saw them years ago, out on the "boleada," riding towards some "pingo" paradise, twisting "las tres Marias" round their heads, bent just a little sideways in the saddle, as, at full speed, they plunged through the pajonales, flitted across the stony wastes, sped through the oceans of brown grass, and disappeared out on the Pampa as a ship slowly sinks into the shadow of the world upon the sea.

EL LAZO

The lazo is of great antiquity. It is said to be depicted in the ruins of Nineveh. An early Persian manuscript, preserved in the Escorial, shows a sportsman (whom I suppose royal by his Olympian expression and careless seat) in the act of catching a wild ass with a nicely plaited rope. The monarch bestrides a rather stocky-looking, dark-coloured horse, with four white feet and a white face. A bow, quiver and a sabre are hung from his saddle, and a sort of housing half covers the horse. How the wild ass is to be restrained, even by the hand of a monarch, is not at first sight evident, for the lazo is neither fixed to the saddle after the fashion of the Gauchos, nor is a half-turn taken round the pommel, in the style adopted by Vaqueros in Mexico and Texas. Apart from this detail, all is as realistically set forth as it would be to-day in a photograph. The horse bears away from the beast lazoed, and the king sits a little to one side, exactly as a Texan Cowboy or an Argentine Gaucho sits under similar circumstances. Irises and narcissi spring up under the horse's feet, and an applauding group of angels peep out of a cloud, whilst in the middle distance another Persian Gaucho shoots an antelope with an arrow whilst galloping at full speed.

One could have wished that the lazo had been depicted nearer to the ass's head, for hanging as it does, just on the withers, the line of most resistance (so dear to monarchs) has evidently been adopted.

The Laplanders are said to lazo their reindeer, and the Tartars and modern Australians use a rudimentary lazo fixed to a long pole in order to catch wild or refractory horses. The Poles, Croatians, and Wallachians, with the Hungarians, seem to have used the lazo till about the beginning of the present century. A picture by the German artist, Richter, shows Polish remounts for the German cavalry being lazoed in the Zwinger at Dresden. The horses look as wild as a Texan "bronco" or an Argentine "bagual," and the attitude of men and animals, and the way the ropes are coiled and thrown, are identical with those adopted in Spanish America to-day. The lazo appears to run through a ring in the pommel of the saddle.

It is, however, in Spanish America where the art has been most developed. This is on account of the open country and the vast numbers of wild and semi-wild horses which, up to the middle of the present century overspread its plains. The lazo may be said to have two great schools: one the style adopted in the Argentine Republic, and the other what may be called the school of Mexico. The Argentine Gaucho and the Brazilian of the province of Rio Grande use a raw-hide lazo, plaited generally in four till within about eight or ten feet of the end, where the plaiting is usually of six, eight, or ten strands, as fancy leads. The lazo terminates in a strong iron ring, which is spliced into the hide so as to remain stiff, and stick out in a straight line from the rope. At the end kept in the hand or attached to the saddle a Turk's head and plaited loop form the finishing. The thickness of the lazo is about that of the little finger, and the hide is kept soft and pliable by frequent applications of grease, for which purpose a piece of raw mutton fat is found to answer best. The Indians use mare's grease, but bacon, oil, or any salted grease is said to burn the hide. To make a lazo the hide of a cow is procured, denuded of hair, and the various strands are softened, either by beating with a mallet or being run through an iron ring, or worked between a piece of split wood (called a "Mordaza"). When properly softened, the inside of the hide is as white as flour, and, if well cared for, will last soft for many years. The ordinary length of an Argentine lazo is about sixty-six feet, though exceptionally tall and powerful men sometimes use lazos of eighty and even ninety feet in length.

A skilful man on foot will catch a horse in a corral at the distance of ten or twelve yards, throwing at the neck. At ten yards he will secure the two fore feet, or a fore and a hind foot, both hind feet, or, catching the animal round the neck, will, by imparting a vibratory motion to the rope, place a half-hitch round the nose, thus forming what is called a "medio bozal," or half-halter. To catch the feet is called "pialar" from *pie*, a foot. The effect of catching by the feet is to throw the animal violently to the ground. Catching round the neck chokes the animal to the ground, if enough force is used. In either case, the moment the lazo tightens, the lazoer throws himself back on the rope, like a seaman hauling on a sheet, and, digging his heels into the ground, bears heavily on the rope with his left hand, which he puts as far behind his back as possible. The strain is most severe, cutting the unaccustomed hand and destroying the clothes, so that in many cases a leather apron is worn to keep off the chafe. A strong colt of five years old will drag three or four men round a corral, if they try to stop him by sheer strength, and the lazo be not tightened high on the neck near the ears; but a boy of sixteen, used to the work, by watching his opportunity, will easily stop the same animal.

To throw a long lazo, height is of great advantage, as, other things being equal, a tall man can throw a longer lazo than a man of low stature. The lazo is prepared for throwing by making a noose from two and a half to four yards in circumference at the ring end of the rope. The ring should be slipped down to about a third of the circumference of the noose. The remainder of the rope is coiled, and two or three coils taken into the right hand together with the noose; the rest of the coils are held in the left hand. Care must be observed not to leave too much slack rope between the coils in the right and left hands, as it is apt to get entangled when the lazo leaves the hand, especially on horseback. Swinging the noose as many times round the head as is required to give the sufficient momentum, and taking care that the noose flies open and with a slight upward inclination, it is then let go, rather than thrown, when the hand is just above the head on the right side, and slides through the air, uncoiling as it flies.

Like throwing a fly, putting screw on a ball at billiards, and taking a close counter of carte, it is an art not easily described, and best learnt by demonstration and by practice.

To become a perfect lazoer (the Spanish word is *enlazador*), the lazo must have been familiar to the thrower from his youth. To be

able to catch a horse in a corral round the neck, with some certainty, can be learnt in about six months by a young and active man accustomed to athletic exercises.

The lazo on horseback is a very different and far more dangerous affair. Accidents are frequent and often fatal, and the business should not be attempted by any one who has not learnt the art in youth. In all cattle districts, in both North and South America, men maimed with the lazo – having lost either fingers, or a hand, or foot – are as common as "mainsheet men" used to be in seaport towns in the days of "windjammers."

The lazo on horseback can be used with far greater effect than on foot. From sixteen to eighteen yards is a fair distance at which to catch an animal when going at full speed. The faster the horse is going, the more easily is the rope thrown; and of course the danger increases in the same ratio. The method of casting on horseback is precisely similar to that used on foot. A larger loop or noose (called *armada* in Spanish) can be used, and care must be taken not to entangle the coils of the "slack" with the reins, or to catch the horse's hind legs, or head, or his fore feet, or to touch him anywhere with the rope, unless he is extremely tame and tractable. For this reason a less elevation must be given to the point of the noose, as it gyrates round the head, on horseback than on foot; that is to say, it should be swung almost level round the head before casting. The end of the lazo retained by the thrower is buttoned into a strong iron ring fixed behind the rider's right thigh to a piece of hide about three inches in length, which piece of hide is firmly sewn into the ring of the upper part of the strong hide surcingale which forms the girth of the Argentine saddle.

This saddle is called *el recado*; it is a modification of the old "Bur" saddle of the time of Charles V., and is known as *albarda* to the Spaniards and *barda* to the Moors. It is composed of several pieces, and surmounted by a rug or sheepskin; the stirrups are hung long, from the middle of the saddle, and are so small as only to admit the toes. The Spaniards anciently called riding in this saddle "riding *à la brida*" as opposed to the short stirrups and high pommel and cantle of the Moorish saddle, which style of riding was called "*à la gineta.*" The Mexican saddle has grown out of this latter style, the stirrups having been lengthened in order to facilitate mounting, and sticking to a wild horse.

When the lazo has been thrown on horseback, and the animal caught round the neck or horns, the difficulty and danger begin. Should the quarry be a wild horse or mare, care has to be taken not to let it cross either in front or behind of the mounted horse. If it does so, there is great danger of a half-turn being taken in the rider's arm or leg, or even a whole turn round his body. The least that can happen is that the mounted horse gets entangled in the rope, becomes frightened, and an accident is almost certain.

Should the animal captured be a bull or cow, the rider must manage to avoid having his horse charged, and for this purpose immediately the noose settles round the beast's horns, the horseman should turn to the near side, i.e., away from the animal lazoed, and endeavour to keep the rope always taut. If he succeeds in doing this, there is little danger of the strongest bull pulling over even a light horse; for it is to be remembered that the weight of the saddle and the rider is an assistance to the horse, as making his weight more nearly equal to that of the bull.

It must not be forgotten that in lazoing on horseback it is the horse that works and holds the animal caught; the rider merely throws the lazo, as no strength of his could hold an animal galloping at full speed. Some horses become so dexterous that the rider can slip off, leaving them to keep the lazo taut, and, approaching the bull, hamstring it, or kill it by plunging a long knife into its neck.

A high-spirited horse that starts, stops, and turns easily, and does not get too much excited, is the best mount for the lazoer. A low-spirited animal exposes its rider to danger from a charging bull, and an excitable horse is apt to get twisted in the coils of the lazo, or by throwing up its head, or swerving as the lazo is delivered, to make the aim defective. In almost every case the lazo is thrown on the off side of the horse (known from that circumstance in South America as the "lazo side"), but now and then a skilful lazoer will throw to the near side, and, catching an animal, pass the rope over his own and his horse's head, or over the quarters of the horse. This process is always attended with danger, and, as the Gauchos say, should not be attempted by married men.

In South America the inhabitants of the Brazilian province of Rio Grande do Sul hold first place for skill with the lazo. After them come the inhabitants of the Republic of Uruguay and the Gauchos of the province of Buenos Ayres.

The Chilians use a slightly different lazo, without a ring, and with a loop and button at both ends. It is twisted in three strands, and known as a "torzal." They are skilful, but, their country being more broken, are inferior to the men on the east side of the Andes.

The second school of lazoers is that of Mexico. There the lazo is never made of hide, but of horsehair of *istlé*, or of the fibre of the aloe. No iron ring is ever used, and the lazo is all one piece, not having an addition spliced on at the end, as in South America.

Being of lighter material, the Mexican lazo cannot be thrown so far as that of the Pampas. It is more easily carried, however, requires no grease, closes more readily on the neck of the animal lazoed, and neither cuts a horse's legs nor a man's hands so severely as a raw-hide rope.

It is on horseback that the difference between the two schools is most manifest. The Mexican lazo is made fast to the saddle in front of the rider, and hence the difficulty of throwing to the off side is largely obviated; as it is easy to pass the lazo over the horse's head and keep the strain on the rope, and hence far fewer accidents occur in Mexico and Texas than in the Pampas. The Mexican system is, however, less effectual against the efforts of a heavy animal, as, the lazo being fastened to the horn of the saddle when an animal is caught, the rope grazes the body of the rider during the process of the struggle, and it appears improbable that the horse can throw as much weight on to the rope as he can under the Argentine system of fastening. It is usual in Mexico not to tie or make fast the end of the lazo to the saddle, but to take a half-hitch round the horn, and hold the end in the left hand. It is considered very dangerous to tie the lazo to the bow of the saddle, and a man who does so is said to *amarrar a muerte* – that is, to tie a death-knot. Mexicans are very dexterous with the lazo on foot, as, owing to the lightness of their rope, it is very easily thrown. Texans, Kansans, and men of the North-West often use a common hemp rope without a ring or button, but merely tie a bowline, and pass the coil of the rope through a bight to form a noose. Texan cowboys are often extremely skilful, performing as many feats with the lazo as the Mexicans or Gauchos, but seldom equalling the Brazilians of Rio Grande, who are the smartest men with lazo or bolas, or on a wild horse, that I have seen.

The lazo, with the bolas, the boomerang, the spear, and bow, in a few years will be but memories. Rifle and gun will have replaced or rendered them unnecessary, and the descendants of the wild riders who mounted "bagual" and "bronco," holding them by the ear, and getting to their seats as a bird lights upon a bough, will wait to catch the tramcar at the corner of the street. Therefore this short description may have its interest, being a sort of record of a dream, dreamed upon pampas and on prairies, sleeping upon a saddle under the southern stars, or galloping across the plains in the hot sun, photographed in youth upon the writer's brain, and, when recalled, more vivid than affairs of State which happened yesterday.

AUNT ELEANOR

There are no aunts to-day like my Aunt Eleanor. Either the world is no more fitted for them, or else they are not fitted to the world; but none of them remain.

Scotland and Yorkshire strove together in her blood, making a compound, whimsical and strange, kind and ungracious, foolish and yet endowed with a shrewd common sense, which kept her safe, during the lengthened period of her life, from all the larger follies, whilst still permitting her to give full run to minor eccentricities, both in speech, deed and dress.

Tall, thin, and willowy, and with a skin like parchment, which gave her face, when worked upon by a slight rictus in the nose she suffered from, a look, as if a horse about to kick, she had an air, when you first saw her, almost disquieting, it was so different from anything, or anybody that you had ever met.

She never seemed to age, although no doubt time did not stop the clock for her during the thirty years she was a landmark in my life. Perhaps it was her glossy, dark brown hair, which, parted in the middle and kept in place by a thin band of velvet, never was tinged with grey, not even in extreme old age, that made her ever young.

Perhaps it was her clothes, which for those five-and-thirty years (I cannot swear it was not forty) were invariable, that made her never change.

Her uniform, for so I styled it, it was so steadfast, was, in the winter, a black silk, sprigged, as she would have said herself, with little trees, and in the summer, on fine days, a lilac poplin, which she called "laylock," surmounted by a Rampore Chudda immaculately white.

Her cap was generally adorned with cherry-coloured ribbons. Perched on her head, as if it were a crown, moral and physical, of virginity, it used to have a strange attraction for me when it trembled, now and then, making the ribbons shake, as she reproved a servant, or signified her disapproval of some necessary change. The youngest of a large family, whose members all were cleverer than she, until death set her free by taking off her sisters, she had been held a fool. Not that the imputation ever stopped her for a moment from having her own way; but only laid her open to the comments of the other members of the family, which she accepted, just as a shepherd or a sailor always accepts bad weather, without a murmur, and with a sense as of superiority to fate.

In all her sisters the Scottish strain prevailed. They spoke, not in broad Scots, but with the intonation that sounds like the whine a bagpipe gives when the player, after a pibroch, or a lament, allows the bag to empty slowly of the wind. Their mental attitude was that which their stern Scottish faith gave to its votaries. Even in Scotland it is now unknown, leaving the world the poorer by the extinction of a type of mind so much at home with the divinity, that it could venture freely to admonish him if he fell short in any of his deeds, from the full standard of perfection raised by his worshippers. So did an ancient Scottish lady on being told, during the course of a dispute on "Sabbath recreation," that the Lord walked in the fields and ate the ears of corn, not hesitate to say, "I ken that weel, and dinna think the mair of Him for that, so I'm just tellin' ye."

Aunt Eleanor was of another leaven, for in her composition the Yorkshire blood had over-powered the Scotch. Reared in the lowest section of the English Church, she used to go occasionally into a Methodist or Baptist chapel, alleging that she had no terror of dissent, although it may have been she looked on the adventure as in the light of dissipation, just as an Arab, now and then, might eat a piece of pork, being convinced his faith was steadfast, but wishing, as it were, to taste the wickedness of sin, to make it manifest.

In the same way, her caprice satisfied, Aunt Eleanor returned again to church, but always used to treat the institution as if it were a sort of appanage belonging to the county families. She used to send and ask the clergyman to tell the organist not to pull out the Vox Humana stop, which she alleged made her feel ill, and never to allow his instrument to groan at her as she came into church.

On ritual she was a bar of iron, not liking what she called "high-flyers," and stating roundly that for her part she would not mind if the "man" stood up to preach in his shirt-sleeves, as long as they were clean.

These were, as far as I remember, all the religious difficulties Aunt Eleanor had to contend with, for in the practice of her creed she was as upright, kind and charitable a Christian as ever I have met. Not that her faith softened a certain harshness in her mind, that made her singularly harsh to all the failings of her sex in matters sexual.

On those of men, she looked with much more leniency, holding that women always were the tempters, and that no girl had ever gone astray except by her own fault.

Once, and once only, did she almost have the chance to put her doctrines into practice, but then the issue was confused, so that it never was cleared up, whether my aunt was better than her creed, or if she held her Scoto-Yorkshire faith in its entirety. A celebrated lady horse-breaker, of perhaps easy virtue, having come into the street in which she lived, my aunt, to the blank consternation of her friends, prepared to strike up an acquaintanceship, and when remonstrated with, observed: "She may be all you say, my dear, but what a seat she has and hands like air; she must have learned in a good school, she rides so quietly."

As fortune willed it, the acquaintanceship was never formed, but had it been, my aunt, I fancy, would have discoursed on snaffles and on curbs, and on that symbol of all equitation, the sacred lipstrap, with as much gusto as she used to do with other of her friends. Strange as it may appear, although a semi-invalid from her birth up, a martyr as she was to violent sick headaches, which in those days were the equivalent of "nerves," she always used to ride.

She and her brother were both horsemen, riding to hounds, and jealous to a fault. No woman, in my aunt's eyes, could ever ride, that is to say, up to her standard. Either their hands were bad, or else their seats were loose, or if both hands and seats were good, they had no nerve, or as a last resort, rode to attract attention. "You know," she used to say, "Miss Featherstone never was known to jump a fence, unless a man was looking at her. If there was but a butcher's boy she would have risked her neck, although, in that long run, the one I told you of, when we met at the Rising Sun upon Edge Hill, and finished somewhere down in Gloucestershire, she never took a fence, and then came up just as we killed, with several officers, all galloping like tailors on the road."

I hear her now, talking about her celebrated mare, "The Little Wonder," which she declared she never touched with a whip in all her life, but once, and never with the spur. This happened at a fence, at which the mare had swerved; but when she felt the whip, she put her back up and entirely refused. A Frenchman who was following my aunt, passed her, and took his hat off, saying as he passed, "Thank you for whip' your mare. I have followed you a month, but never pass you till to-day." My aunt never related this, but tears rose in her eyes: whether at her own cruelty, or at the Frenchman having passed her, I never could make out.

Horses and hunting were the chief themes of conversation with my aunt, and as she did not care the least for anyone's opinion but her own, her talk ran usually into a monologue, in which she set her theories out, as to which rein should go under which finger, and how good hands consisted in the wrist. "It is all done with a turn of the wrist, my dear, and not by butchering," a theory sound in itself and one which many would be wise to follow, if they had aunts as competent as mine to teach them the right way. Years only added to my aunt's eccentricity, and as she lived in times when gentlewomen enjoyed ill-health, no one was much astonished when one day she definitely took to a couch, laid in the drawing-room window, from which she could survey the road and watch the people going to the meet.

For years she lay there, only getting up on Sunday to go to church, which she did, either in a Bath chair, or else in Jackson's fly, for she averred that only Jackson in the whole town of Leamington could drive with decency. The other flymen started with a jerk, or sawed their horses' mouths in a way that set my aunt's nerves tingling, and used to make her open the window and expostulate in a high, quavering key. Even the trusted Jackson had to submit to adverse criticism now and then, both of his driving and of his horse's legs.

It used to be a curious sight to see the semi-invalid, leaning upon her maid, dressed in her invariable black, sprigged silk gown – she would have fainted to have heard it called a dress – a curtain bonnet on her head, a parasol ringed with small flounces and jointed in the middle, in her hand, walk down the steps of her front door and stand before the fly.

Turning towards her maid, she used to say, "Baker, lend me your arm a moment," and then advancing with the half valetudinarian, half sporting air that she affected, open the horse's mouth.

"Well, Jackson," she would say, "you have got a young one there. I think he would make a better hunter than some of those I see trotting down to the meet. They breed them far too long-backed nowadays, not like the well-ribbed-up, short-legged, well-coupled-up ones that I remember when I hunted as a girl with the Fitzwilliam hounds."

Jackson would touch his hat, and answer, "You know a 'orse, Miss, and this one, 'e is a 'orse, he ought by rights to be a gentleman's."

Then with an admonition as to not starting with a jerk, my aunt would get into the fly, Baker having first put in a coonskin cushion with the head on, made in the fashion of a pillow-case.

Into it when my aunt had put her feet, arranged her shawl and her belongings carefully about her, just as if she were going on a journey in the wilds, the fly rolled off upon its way, with my aunt looking out now and then to criticise the driver and the horse. After having lain upon her couch ten years or so, one day she suddenly got up. The ensuing week she went out hunting, dressed in her long Victorian habit, tall hat and veil, and with a boa round her neck. She hunted on, riding much harder than most members of the hunt, but in a modest and retiring way, and followed by her groom. He, a staid lad, who had been brought up with Lord Fitzwilliam as an under-strapper in the hunt stables, always used to say: "Them as rides with my lady 'as to know 'ow to ride; but then I passed my youth with Lord Fitzwilliam. They was a serious family, all rode to 'ounds, and all of 'em rode blood 'orses, from the old lord down to the little gals."

My aunt continued riding to extreme old age, and then went to the meets driven in a fly, of course, by someone she could put her trust in, though Jackson long had passed away, to drive perhaps in some particular limbo, where the shades of Captain Barclay, old Squire Osbaldiston, and Sir Tatton Sykes drove shadowy chariots, dressed in their "down the road" coats, with a coach and horses on the big pearl buttons, just as they had appeared in life, all with straws in the corners of their mouths, and with that air of supernatural knowledge of the horse which they all had on earth.

My aunt, I fancy, could she have chosen for herself, would have gone to some heaven, half stable and half country house, with just a sprinkling of Low Church divines flying about in black Geneva gowns and white lawn bands, to give an air of having been redeemed, to the select, but rather scanty, inmates of the place when they sat down to dine.

Poor lady, all her life was one long tutelage, till her last sister died. Then when she had peeped below the blinds to satisfy herelf that the hearse horses all were sound, and none wore housings, a thing that she detested, saying she could not bear to see a horse in petticoats, she found herself quite free.

After the fashion of the times, she did not go herself to see her sister buried, but sat at home and read the Burial Service, although a member of the family averred on his return he caught her dozing with the Church Service closed upon her lap, and *Market Harboro'* in her hand. Years passed, and she became a kindly tyrant in her old age, making her young relations happy and terrified by her ungracious kindness to them all.

Lastly, in a Bath chair, she used to have herself dragged up and down the Holly Walk or the Parade, criticising horses and riders most relentlessly, and now and then making the chairman stop before the shops where pictures were for sale, and after looking at them most intently, usually saying, " 'Tis distance lends enchantment to the view," a piece of criticism which she thought final, as applied to art in all its branches, even to photographs.

She died as she had lived, after arranging her own funeral with the undertaker, and enjoining on him to be sure that the hearse was not started with a jerk, and all his beasts were sound.

He left her presence snorting a little in a bandanna pocket-handkerchief, remarking: "Well, I never saw such a lady in my life, a plucked one to be sure, I'll bet a suvering."

My aunt rests quietly under some elm trees in Old Milverton churchyard.

Many old Scottish ladies lie round about the grave where my aunt sleeps under a granite slab now stained a little with the weather, imparting to the churchyard a familiar air, as of the tea-parties that she once used to give, when they all sat together, just as they now lie closely in the ground, to keep each other warm. The rooks caw overhead, and when the hounds pass on a bright November morning, I hope she hears them, for heaven would be to her but a dull dwelling-place if it contained no horses and no hounds.

SNAEKOLL'S SAGA

Thorgrimur Hjaltalin was known throughout all Rangarvallar, down to Krusavik, up to Akureyri, and in fact all over Iceland, for his wandering disposition, his knowledge of the Sagas, and for his horse called "Snaekoll." He lived in Upper Horgsdalr, near the Skaptar Jokull, and from his green "tun" were seen the peaks of Skaptar Jokull, Orœfar, and the white cordillera of the vast icy Vatna.

A Scandinavian of the Scandinavians, Thorgrimur was tall and angular, red-bearded, yellow-haired, grey-eyed, and as deliberate in all his movements as befits an Icelander, compared to whom the Spaniards, Turks, Chinese, or Cholos of the Sierras of Peru are active, quick in design and movement, and mercurial in mind.

His house was built of Norway pine with door jambs of hard wood, floated almost to his home from the New World. Unlike most Icelanders, he had not profited too much by education, leaving Greek, Latin, and the "humanities" in general for those who liked them; but of the Sagas he was passionately fond, reading and learning them by heart, copying them out of books in the long evenings whilst his family sat working round the lamp on winter nights after the fashion of their land.

People were wont to say he was descended from some Berserker, he was so silent and yet so subject to sudden fits of passion, which came on generally after a fit of laughter, ending in wrath or tears. Berserkers, not a few, had lived in Rangarvallar, and it may be that moral qualities become endemic in localities, in the same way that practices still cling to places, as in Rome and Oxford and some other towns where the air seems vitiated by the breath of generations long gone past.

Thus, in the future, when the taint of commerce has been purged away and the world cleansed from all the baseness commerce brings, it may be that for some generations those born in London, Liverpool, in Glasgow and New York, will for a time be more dishonest than their fellows born in cities where trade did not so greatly flourish, and so of other things.

Thorgrimur was married and had children, as he had sheep, cattle, poultry, dogs, and all the other requisites of country life. But wife and children occupied but little of his mind, though after the fashion of his countrymen he was kind and gentle to them, sought no other women, did not get drunk, gamble, or regulate his conduct upon the pattern of the husbands of more favoured lands. All his delight was to read Sagas, to dream of expeditions through the great deserts of his country, and his chief care was centred in his horses, and most especially in "Snaekoll," his favourite, known, like himself, for his peculiarities.

Whilst there are camels in the desert, llamas in Peru, reindeer in Lapland, dogs in Greenland, and caiques amongst the Esquimaux, Iceland will have its ponies, who on those "Pampas of the North" will still perform the services done by the mustangs of the plains of Mexico, the horses of the Tartars, Gauchos, and even more than is performed by any animal throughout the world. Without the ponies Iceland would be impossible to live in, and when the last expires the Icelanders have two alternatives – either to emigrate *en masse*, or to construct a system of highways for bicycles, an undertaking compared to which all undertaken by the Romans and the Incas of Peru in the same sphere would be as nothing.

No Icelander will walk a step if he can help it; when he dismounts he waddles like an alligator on land, a Texan cowboy, or a Gaucho left "afoot," or like the Medes whom Plutarch represents as tottering on their toes when they dismounted from their saddles and essayed to walk. Ponies are carts, are sledges, carriages, trains – in short, are locomotion and the only means of transport: bales of salt fish, packages of goods, timber projecting yards above their heads and trailing on the ground behind like Indian lodge poles, they convey across the rocky lava tracks. The farmer and his wife, his children, servants, the priest, the doctor, "Syselman," all ride, cross rivers on the ponies' backs, plunge through the snow, slide on the icy "Jokull" paths, and when the lonely dweller of some upland dale expires, his pony bears his body in its coffin tied to its back, to the next con- secrated ground.

So Thorgrimur loved "Snaekoll," and was proud of all his qualities, his size, for "Snaekoll" almost attained to fourteen hands, a giant stature amongst the ponies of his race. In colour he was iron-grey, with a white foot on either side, so that his rider had the satisfaction of riding on a cross, fierce-tempered, bad to mount, a kicker at the stirrup, biter, unrideable by strangers, but, as Thorgrimur said, an "ice-eater"; that is, able to live on nothing and dig for lichens on the rocks when snow lay deep, to feed upon salt cod or on dried whale beef, and for that reason not quite safe to leave alone with sheep when they had lambs. But for all that Thorgrimur did not care, and never grudged a lamb or two when he reflected that his horse could go his fifty miles a day for a whole week, and at the end be just as fresh as when he left the "tun."

Thick-necked, stiff-jawed, straight pasterns high in the withers, square in the croup, mane like a bottle-brush, tail long and thick, "Snaekoll" had certainly few points of beauty: still, as he stood nodding beneath his Danish saddle, hobbled with whale-hide hobbles, shod with shoes made by Thorgrimur himself, stuck full of large round-headed nails and made long at the heel and curving up near to the coronet to protect his feet in crossing lava-fields, he had a gleam in his red eyes like a bull terrier, which warned the stranger not to come too near. This was a source of pride to Thorgrimur, who used to say, with many quite superfluous "hellvites," that his horse was fit for "Grettir, Burnt Njal, or Viga Glum to ride;" then, mounting him, he used to dash full speed over a lava field, sending a shower of sparks under his feet, cracking his whale-hide whip, and stopping "Snaekoll" with a jerk whilst sitting loosely with his legs stuck out after the fashion of all horsemen when they know they are observed.

Smaakoll's Saga.

To cross the Vatna Jokull, the great icy desert, which extends between the top of Rangarvallar and the east coast of Berufjördr, was Thorgrimur's day-dream. Others had journeyed over deserts, crossed Jokulls, as the icy upland wastes of Iceland are called, but in his time no one had yet been found to cross the Vatna. Now this idea was ever present in his brain during his lonely rides in summer from his home to Reykjavik, from thence to Krusavik, or as he jogged across the lava-fields or crossed the tracts on which grew birch and mountain ash a foot in height, which constitute an Icelandic forest; and in the winter, in the long, dark hours, he could not drive it from his head. Men came to laugh at him, as men will laugh at those who have ideas of any kind, and call him "Thorgrimur of Vatna Jokull, the Berserker of Rangarvallar," and the like, but none laughed openly, for Thorgrimur was hasty in his wrath, and apt to draw his whale knife, or at least spur his horse "Snaekoll" at the laugher's horse, as he had been a fighter in the ancient horse fights, and it was lucky if the horse that "Snaekoll" set upon escaped without some hurt.

In fact the man was a survival, or at the least an instance, of atavism strongly developed, or would have been so styled in England; but in Iceland all such niceties were not observed, and his compatriots merely called him mad, being convinced of their own sanity, as men who make good wages, go to church, observe the weather and the stocks, read books for pastime, marry and have large families, pay such debts as the law forces them to pay, and never think on abstract matters, always are convinced in every land.

Think on the matter for a moment, and at once it is apparent they are right.

The world is to the weak. The weak are the majority. The weak of brain, of body, the knock-kneed and flat-footed, muddle-minded, loose-jointed, ill-put-together, baboon-faced, the white-eye-lashed, slow of wit, the practical, the unimaginative, forgetful, selfish, dense, the stupid, fatuous, the "candle-moulded," give us our laws, impose their standard on us, their ethics, their philosophy, canon of art, literary style, their jingling music, vapid plays, their dock-tailed horses, coats with buttons in the middle of the back; their hideous fashions, aniline colours, their Leaders, Leightons, Logsdails; their false morality, their supplemented monogamic marriage, social injustice done to women; legal injustice that men endure, making them fearful of the law, even with a good case when the opponent is a woman; in sum, the monstrous ineptitude of modern life with all its inequalities, its meannesses, its petty miseries, contagious diseases, its drink, its gambling, Grundy, Stock Exchange, and terror of itself, we owe to those, our pug-nosed brothers in the Lord, under whose rule we live.

Wise Providence, no doubt, has thus ordained it, so that each one of us can see the folly of mankind, and fancy that ourselves alone are strong, are wise, are prudent, faithful, handsome, artistic, to be loved, are poets (with the gift of rhyme left out), critics of music, literature, of eloquence, good business men and generally so constituted as to be fit to rule mankind had not some cursed spite, to man's great detriment, cozened us out of our just due. So Thorgrimur was mad, and pondered on the crossing of the Vatna, day by day; not that he thought of profit or of fame – your true explorer thinks of neither. But like a wild goose making north in spring, or as a swallow flying south without a chart to shape his voyage by; or as a Seychelle cocoanut adrift upon some oceanic current all unknown to it, your true explorer must explore, just as the painter paints, the poet sings, or as the sworn Salvationist must try to save a soul, and in the trying lose perhaps his only friend – a perilous business when one thinks that souls are many, friends are few.

And still the Vatna Jokull filled Thorgrimur's imagination. Surely, to be alone in those great deserts would be wonderful, the stars must needs look brighter so far away from houses, the grass in the lone valleys greener where no animal had cropped it, and then to sleep alone with "Snaekoll" securely hobbled, feeding near at hand; and, lastly – for Thorgrimur was not devoid of true icelandic pride – the arrival one fine morning at the first houses above Berufjördr, calling for milk at the farm door, and saying airily, in answer to the inquiry from whence he came, from Rangarvallar, across the Vatna. That would indeed be worth a lifetime of mere living, after all.

Needless to say that no one in the time of Thorgrimur had ever passed over the Vatna from Rangarvallar, though the Heimskringla seemed to indicate that at the first settlement there had been such a road. Reindeer were known to haunt the wild recesses of the desert track, and some said, ponies long escaped had there run wild, and all were well aware that evil spirits haunted the valleys, for there the older gods had all retired when Christianity had triumphed in the land.

Two hundred miles in distance, but then the miles were mortal, without food, perhaps no water, without a guide, except the compass and the stars. Seven days' ride on "Snaekoll," if all went well, and if it did not, why then as well to sleep alone amongst the mountains, as in the fat churchyard, for there men when they see your headstone growing green forget you, but he who dies in the lone Vatna surely keeps his memory ever fresh.

All through the winter, Thorgrimur talked ceaselessly about the execution of his dream. In spring, when grass is green and horses fat, when forests of dwarf birch and willow look like fields of corn, ice disappears and valleys as by magic are all clothed with grass, he made all boune to set out on his long-projected ride. "Snaekoll is eight years old (he said) and in his prime, sound both in wind and limb, and I am thirty, and if we cannot now prove ourselves of the true Icelandic breed the time will never come, old age will catch us both still scheming, still a-planning, and men will say that had we lived among the Icelanders of old, Snaekoll had been of no use at the horse-fighting, and I, instead of going a sea-roaming with Viga Glum, with Harold Fair-Hair, Askarpillir, with Asgrim, and the rest, would have remained at home and helped the women spin." His wife, after the practical way of womenkind, thought him a fool, but yet admired him, for she imagined that Thorgrimur in reading Sagas had come upon the whereabouts of some great treasure buried in times gone by, for she could not imagine that a man would risk his life without good reason, being all unaware that generally lives are risked and lost without a cause. Perhaps, too, she was willing enough for Thorgrimur to go, his musings, readings, wanderings, and uncanny ways rendering him an unpleasant inmate of the house.

But Thorgrimur cared nothing, or perhaps knew nothing of her speculations, but got his saddle freshly stuffed, made whale-hide reins strong, new, and six feet long; purveyed a long hair rope, new hobbles, and for himself new whale-hide shoes like Indians' mocassins, new wadmal clothes, and laid up a provision of salt fish and rye-flour bread all ready for the start.

News travels fast in Iceland, as it does in Arabia, the Steppes of Russia, in Patagonia and other countries where there are no newspapers and where wayfaring men, even though fools, pass news along with such rapidity that it appears there is no need of telegraphs or telephones, for what is done in one part of the land to-day is known to-morrow miles away, and just as much distorted as it had been disseminated through the medium of the Press. Thus Rangarvallar and all southern Iceland knew of Thorgrimur's intention, and people came from far and near to visit him, for time in Iceland is held valuable, or at the least folk think it so, and, therefore, spend what they prize most after the fashion that most pleases them, and that by talking ceaselessly, mostly of nothing, though they can work as patiently as beavers, when they choose. And thus it came about that at the little church in Upper Horgsdalr a crowd of neighbours had assembled to see the start of Thorgrimur into the unknown wastes.

To say the truth the church was of as mean a presence as was the author of the most part of the faith expounded in its walls. Built all of rubble, roof of Norway pine, the little shingled steeple shaped like a radish, nothing about the building, but the bell cast centuries ago in Denmark, could be called beautiful; but still it served its turn and as a mosque in a lone "duar" in Morocco, stood always open for the faithful to use by day for prayer, and as a sleeping-place at night. In the churchyard, curiously marked and patterned stones bore witness to the supposititious virtues of those long dead, and from the mound on which the church was built, the view extended far across lava-fields over the reddish mountains flecked here and there with green and crowned with snow, and in the distance rose the glaciers and the peaks of the unknown and icy Vatna. A landscape dreary in itself, unclothed by trees, wild, desolate, and only beautiful when the sun's rays transformed it, turning the peaks to castles, blotting the black and ragged lava out, and blending all into a vast prismatic play of colour, changing and shifting as the lights ran over limestone, rested on basalt, and lit the granite of the cliffs, making each smallest particle to shine like mica in a piece of quartz. The Icelanders do not hold Sunday as a day of gloom, devoted, as it used to be in England and still remains in the remoter parts of Scotland to which the beneficent breath of latter-day indifference has not yet penetrated, sacred to prayer and drink. So Sunday was the day on which Thorgrimur intended to set out; dressed in his best he sat at church, his wife and children seated by his side. The service done, he left the church, and pushing through the ponies all waiting for their owners outside the door, entered his house.

The priest, the "Syselman," the notables, and friends from far and near sat down to dine, and dinner over and the corn brandy duly circulating, Thorgrimur rose up to speak. "My friends, and you the priest and 'Syselman,' and you the notables, and neighbours who have known me from a boy, I drink your health. I go to try what I have dreamed of all my life; whether I shall succeed no man can tell, but still I shall succeed so far in that I have had the opportunity to follow out my dream. I hold that dreams are the reality of life and that which men call practical, that which down there in Reykjavik the folk call business, is but a dream. 'Snaekoll' and I depart to cross the Vatna, perhaps not to return, but still to try, and so I drink your health again and say farewell, 'Skoal,' to you all."

Then mounting "Snaekoll," who stood arching up his back, he kissed his wife, and saying to his children, "Stand aside, for 'Snaekoll' bites worse than a walrus," he took the road. His friends rode with him for a "thingmanslied" upon the way, and when the last few scattered farms were passed and the track ended in a rising lava-field stretching to the hills, bade him God-speed and watched him sitting erect on "Snaekoll" fade into nothing upon the lava-fields, his horse first sinking out of sight and then his body, bit by bit, till he was gone. The priest, spurring his horse upon a rocky hill, claimed to have seen him last, and said that Thorgrimur never once looked behind, but rode into the desert as he was riding to his home, and that he fancied as he saw him ride, he saw the last of the old Berserks disappear. And then the Vatna claimed him, and Thorgrimur of Rangarvallar went his way out of this story and the world's.

But in east Berufjördr, not far from Hargifoss, there dwelt one Hiörtr Helagson, a man of substance, owner of flocks and herds, and as he sat one morning at his "baer" door, drinking his coffee sweetened with lumps of sugar-candy in the Icelandic fashion, waiting until his horse was caught to ride to church, his herdsman entered to inform him that he thought "Hellvite," the devil had got amongst the horses, for he said, "they run about as if in fear, and the dark chestnut which you ride has a piece bitten out of his back as by a wolf." Then Hiörtr Helagson, although the "Syselman" of Berufjördr and elder of the Church, swore like a horseman when he knows his horse is sick or come by mischief, and, taking down his gun, went to the pasture where his horses fed. The horses all were running to and fro like sheep, and in the corner of the field an object lay, dark grey in colour, like a Greenland bear. But when the "Syselman" had raised his gun, it staggered to its feet, and he, on looking at it, said to his herdsman,

"Ansgottes, this is the horse of Thorgrimur of Rangarvallar; he must be dead amongst the ice-fields, and his horse has wandered here." Time passed and "Snaekoll" once again grew round and sleek, although a pest to all the horses in the "tun," and Hiörtr, thinking to cut a figure at a cattle fair, saddled and mounted him. "Snaekoll" stood still, though looking backwards, and when the "Syselman" was seated on his back, arching his spine, the horse plunged violently, and coming down with legs as stiff as posts, gave Hiörtr Helagson a heavy fall, and – turning on him like a tiger – would have killed him had not help been nigh. So, from that day, no one essayed to ride the dead man's horse, who ranged about the fields, and, after years, slept with the horses of the Valkyrie. But Hiörtr Helagson had the best ponies in all Berufjördr, hardy, untirable, and "ice-eaters," fiery in spirit, hard to mount, kickers and biters, apt to rear and plunge, fit for the saddle only of such few commentators as can catch the stirrup at the moment they are up. And when the neighbours talked about their temper and their ways, Hiörtr would say, "Well, yes, they are descended from the horse of Thorgrimur of Rangarvallar; his name was "Snaekoll," and he came to me out of the desert, lean as a bear in spring. You know his master died trying to cross the Vatna, and "Snaekoll" how he lived amongst the ice and found his way to Berufjördr, I cannot tell. Up in the Vatna there is naught but ice, and yet he must have eaten something; *what* it was, God knows!"

THE GRAVE OF THE HORSEMAN

A little town just glimmered in the distance, lost in orange groves, with a few date palms waving above the saint's tomb near the gate, their ragged tops looking like seaweed in a pool left by the tide upon the beach. High mountains flanked the road, which ran between great boulders, with here and there flat slabs of whinstone cropping up, shiny and slippery with the heat. A grove of cork trees shadowed it on one side, and at the other the precipitous street of the strange mountain village called Bahallein, with the houses separated by a brawling stream which roared and foamed eternally, ran surging into caverns, and, again emerging into view, made a right angle to its course.

Smoke rose from many of the houses, and a wail of Arab women pierced the noise of the tumultuous stream. A band of horsemen, with a scout or two thrown out on either side, picked their way through the stones, their horses propping themselves on their fore-legs, drawing their quarters after them when they had found a foot-hold, making their riders sway upon their saddles as when a camel rises to its feet. Some of them bore fresh-cut-off heads upon the muzzles of their guns, either stuck stiffly on, as boys stick turnips on a stick, or with a lap of skin left on the throat, through which the gun was thrust, leaving the head to hang down limply like a fish. They drove before them cattle, urging them onwards with their spearlike guns. Occasionally a man stood out upon a rock and fired his long and slender-barrelled gun, which went off sullenly as the rough, home-made powder, ill rammed home, ignited slowly, sending the bullet over the heads of the retiring band. Sometimes a woman stood close to their path, shaking a ragged haik and cursing, and when a horseman passed he turned a little out of his way and rode on with his eyes fixed far away, as if he had seen nothing, leaving her wailing by the road.

They closed their ranks and rode into the track that leads from Fez to Séfru, the scouts falling back on the main body when the last dropping shots of the harried villagers were spent. Horses neighed shrilly, and when they passed mares feeding by the outskirts of the cork wood, danced sideways or plunged into the air, their riders checking them so sharply with the curb that a red foam hung round their mouths as they fell back upon the bit. A cloud of dust hung over all the band, through which at times appeared a horse and rider, the man dressed all in white, save for a long, blue cloak which streamed out in the wind, and the horse saddled with the high-cantled Arab saddle covered with orange silk. Faces tanned to the colour of a boot or white as ivory and set in jet-black beards looked out from under hoods drawn up above their turbans, with here and there a flat-nosed negro, looking still blacker in the white clothes he wore. Black, grey, and chestnut, with roans and piebalds and the mixed colours that the Arabs call "stones of the river," their horses looked as if they had all stepped from pictures by Velazquez, with tails that swept the ground, manes reaching almost to their knees, and forelocks falling to their nostrils, covering their eyes like veils. Their riders, thin and wiry, were of those who live by "clashing of the spurs," as goes the Arab phrase, and their wild eyes appeared to be eternally fixed on the horizon and to see nothing nearer than a mile away. Except the love of blood and pillage, they had but one thing in common — the fear and hatred of their chief, who rode along behind them, swathed to the eyes in white, on which a spot or two of blood served as a sort of trade-mark of his interior grace.

Seated a little heavily upon a chestnut horse with a white tail and mane, Si Omar had returned his gun to its red flannel case, but held it

still across the saddle, balanced against the pommel with an occasional
motion of his hand. His horse reared and plunged forward now and
then, fretting to join the others, but its rider took no notice except to
slack his bridle hand a little, and when the animal came back upon the
bit and gave its head, he threw the long red silken reins across his
shoulder, where they remained, looking as if someone had drawn a
bloody finger down his clothes. His spearlike, single-pointed spurs
hung loosely from his red-and-yellow riding-boots, and just behind
his heavy stirrups damascened with gold, had made a bloody patch
upon his horse's flanks, which he spurred constantly, after the Arab
fashion, to keep him to his pace. Dark, for a Berber, and marked a
little here and there with smallpox, his spare black beard showing the
skin between the hairs, Si Omar looked about forty-five, and had
begun to put on flesh a little, after the fashion of his race when
fortune smiles upon them, although he passed his life on horseback
and in the open air. He wore the lock of hair, hanging down on his
cheek, called by the Berbers "el kettaieh," that gave an air of fierceness
to his face, which his wild eye and ever-twitching mouth accentuated.
His hands were small with the nails clean and cared for, and when he
raised his arm and loose sleeves of his selham left bare his wrist,
slender and nervous, with something of the look as of a leopard's
claw or of the leg of a gazelle. As he rode on he drew a fold of his
selham about his mouth, covering his face, leaving his eyes, bloodshot
and staring, alone exposed to view. Passing the cork wood, the
horsemen, driving their "creagh" slowly in front of them, came out
upon the plain and struck into a road which ran along the foothills
of the mountains, from which the little, glistening town of Séfru
appeared, a league or two away, buried in gardens and in woods. The
sun was slanting towards the west and bathed the plain in a pale glow
which blended everything together, making the pastoral Arab life
a perfect illustration of the Old Testament as we conceive it, in the
glow of the imagination of our faith. Herds lowed, and sheep drawn
out in lines straggled towards the fold, preceded by a boy who piped
upon a reed whose twittering notes hung in the air like the faint echo
of a lark's song when it has soared into the clouds.

The women went and came about the wells dressed in the desert
blue that makes their supple figures look even more slender than they
are, with pointed amphorae upon their shoulders or balanced on
their heads. Foals frisked beside their mothers, and here and there

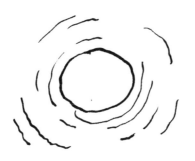

camels stood up outlined against the sky or browsed upon the thorny
bushes, their outstretched necks writhing about like snakes. Elders
sat at the doors of tents in groups, and the whole plain looked peaceful,
happy, and exhaled an air as of eternity, so well the life fitted the
scene and the scene sanctified the life. Above it, the marauding band
passed, as a kite may pass above a dovecote, a wolf prowl past a fold,
or as a train rushes at sixty miles an hour through some quiet valley
in the hills. The horses neighed and passaged, and a cloud of dust
covered the horsemen and the animals they drove, whilst in the rear
the solitary chief rode silent and as if buried in a dream.

The world was going well with him, and the new sultan had
confirmed him in his governorship both of the tribe and of the town.
Indeed he was a man designed by nature to rule over such a tribe as
was Ait Yusi, whose members passed their lives in fighting and in
deeds of violence. His father had ruled them with a rod of iron,
making himself so hated that at last the tribe had risen and burned
him on a pile of hay. He knew himself detested, even by his horsemen,
and for that reason always rode behind them to avoid an accidental
shot, though at the same time all feared him far too much to look him
in the face. So he rode on, cursing his horse when it tripped on a
stone, and muttering the proverb that declares the horseman's grave
is always open when it stumbled in the mud, and keeping a keen eye
on all the thickets for a chance shot from some of his own tribesmen
and on his soldiers whenever they looked back. Still he had passed
his life upon the watch, after the fashion of a tiger, and now he was
content to muse upon the future as his horse paced along the road.
The way seemed open for him to ascend, and the new sultan was on
the look out for men on whom he could rely. Visions of larger
governments rose in his mind, of the great kasbah he would build –
for building is a passion with the Arabs – with courts that led from
courts into more courts, with crenellated walls, a garden with its
clump of cypresses, a mosque, rooms paved with tiles from Fez and
Tetuán, a fishpond full of gold and silver fish, with water everywhere,
gurgling in little rills of white cement beneath the orange trees. He
saw himself all dressed in dazzling white, sitting upon a mattress in a
room open to the court of orange trees, lulled by the murmuring of
the water, drinking green tea flavoured with amber amongst his
women, or talking with his friends, what time his secretary wrote his
letters, in his guest-chamber.

Horses, of course, were plentiful, and all of lucky colours, so that a man when he set off upon a journey might be certain to return. Some should be pacers, for the road, and others for the powder-play, light as gazelles, and bitted so as to turn, just as a seagull turns upon the wing. He felt himself assured of fortune and safe to rise in the good graces of his lord, whilst the declining sun, which fell upon his face, blinding him to the difficulties of the rough track on which he rode, induced a feeling of contentment which perhaps threw him off his guard.

A mare and foal feeding close by had set Si Omar's horse neighing and plunging, and he, swaying a little to the plunges, may perhaps have touched it in the mouth too sharply with the bit. After a spring or two, the horse passaged and reared, and lighting on a flat slab of rock which cropped up in the middle of the road, slipped sideways and fell with a loud crash, its shoes, in the last struggle to maintain its balance, sending a shower of sparks into the air. All passed as if by magic, and the man who but an instant previously had ridden so contentedly lay a crushed mass of draggled white under the horse, which in a moment had regained its feet. He lay pale, but quite conscious, with his hand still clasped upon his rifle, looking up fiercely like a wounded animal awaiting the final stroke. His followers, hearing the noise, turned and surrounded him, glaring down at their wounded chief with hard, unsympathising eyes. Not a word passed on either side, and then a Berber, mounted upon a sorrel colt with four white feet and a large blaze upon its nose, exclaimed, "God wishes it; Si Omar's day is done." Then, slowly levelling his gun, he shot his fallen chieftain through the body at short range, and all the rest, crowding about him as he lay bleeding on the ground, fired into him, spurring their horses over the prostrate body on the ground. Whether Si Omar died of the first shot, or whether, seeing his day was done, he set his teeth and died as a wild boar dies, silently, without a sign, none of his slayers knew. A cloud of dust hung in the air above the spot where men rode furiously about firing their guns and shouting, and then it cleared away, leaving a small, white bundle of torn rags upon the ground stained here and there with blood.

The white-maned chestnut which the dead man had ridden stood grazing quietly a hundred yards away, and the declining sun fell on the stony hill beyond the road, flushing it with a tinge of pinkish yellow, between the colour of an old piece of ivory and a worn

Roman brick. A league away Séfru lay sleeping in its orange groves, and from the plain below the road came up the bleating of the sheep as they were driven to the fold.

The slayers, pressing their Arab stirrups into their horses' sides, rode on a little, and as they passed an angle of the road, settling their flowing robes and loading up their rifles as they went, a Berber turned and, sitting sideways on his horse, fired a last shot at his dead chief, which struck the ground a little short and, flying upwards, flattened the bullet on a rock far up against the hill. The horsemen drew together, as if by instinct, just as a flight of birds collects after some incident which has broken up their ranks, and, swaying in their saddles easily, their long white selhams fluttering in the wind, they disappeared along the road.

TSCHIFFELY'S RIDE

Tschiffely, Mancha and Gato. The three names are as indivisible as the three Persons of the Trinity.

They will go down to history in the Argentine with far more certainty than those of many worthy politicians, gold-laced generals, diplomats, and others who have strutted their brief hour upon the stage of the republic.

Tschiffely in his various letters to the Press during his three years' journey from Buenos Aires to New York, reveals his sympathetic personality.

Writing from Washington, on April 26th, 1928, to "La Asociacion Militar de Retirados del Ejercitoy Armada," Buenos Aires, he signs, "Tschiffely, Mancha y Gato." On other occasions he says, "remembrances and neighs, from the horses."

Tschiffely, a Swiss long settled in the Argentine, a famous horseman, is a man of iron resolution and infinite resource, as his great feat, perhaps the greatest that man and horses have performed in all the history of the world, is there to show.

As to the horses, their deeds speak better for them than any words.

For the last fifty years, it has been the ambition of most stockbreeders in the Argentine to "improve" the native breed of horse, and above all to add a cubit to his stature by taking thought.

They took the thought, and certainly added a cubit (read "hand") to the native horses' height. Nature, however, had her eye upon their work. By crossing with the thoroughbred, the Arab, the Pecheron, the Cleveland Bay and other strains, they bred a taller horse, faster, and fitter both for polo and parade. But strange as it may sound, polo is not the only thing for which horses are designed. It soon was found that the half-bred (mestizo) horse, though larger, faster, and stronger, was a soft animal unfit for work with cattle, slow to jump off the mark, clumsy in turning. . . . At this point, I hear my polo players exclaim, "How can a polo pony be called clumsy at turning round?" True that on a well-levelled polo ground, rolled, watered, and treated almost as a lawn, he lumbers round quite readily. But polo players ride for pleasure, their horses are fed and pampered, almost like "Christians." I use the word, not in the religious, but the Spanish sense.

All that can happen to their riders is a collision, a sudden fall or something of the kind. Most polo players die in their beds, with doctors in attendance, and with the Sacraments of Mother Church, after an old age of drinking cocktails in the club, talking of lip-straps, curbs, martingales, bog and blood spavins, splints and other matters of their mystery. The cattleman rides for his daily bread. His horse eats grass, and he himself, as did "Sir Percivell" (in *The Rhyme of Sir Thopas*), sleeps in his hood (read "poncho") and when on the road drinks, if not "water of the well," the coffee-coloured fluid of some "charco" or "arroyo" of the plains. The cattle peon plunges into a sea of wild-eyed longhorns, or light-footed Hereford, where a false touch upon the reins means a wound; a fall means death. He rides swinging his lazo, over the roughest ground, and that upon a horse that perhaps has not tasted food or water since sunrise, and then, work over, has to march behind a troop of cattle, and sleep tied to a stake, upon the Pampa, in an icy winter's night, or in a scorching north wind that shrivels up the grass. Gradually it dawned upon cattlemen that the half-bred was an inferior animal for such work. He was slow to turn, proved a poor weight-carrier, was unsafe when galloping in rough ground, and a cold night or two, without his blanket and his corn, made a poor horse of him indeed.

So they turned back to nature, and procured some horses of the old native stock from El Cacique Liompichon, an Indian chief in Patagonia, and started the Criollo (native) stud book, for the native horse. It was found fourteen-two or fourteen-three was the best height for work, for taller horses, even of pure native stock, were not so fit to stand long days, short commons and hard work.

Then they set about to put their theories into practice and show the world the wonderful endurance of the Criollo horse. Now it was that the famous trio, Tschiffely, Mancha and Gato, came upon the scene.

As soon as the "Asociacion Criadores de Criollo," with its stud book, was instituted, long distance rides were undertaken, to show what the Criollo horse could do. Don Abelardo Piovano, on his horse, Lunarejo Cardal, covered the distance of eight hundred and fifty-seven miles in seventeen days, from Buenos Aires to Mendoza, carrying about thirteen stone.

This was no ride round some great stadium, with grooms always in attendance with water and with corn, rubbers and bandages, and a warm stable every night. The route ran over open plains, sparsely inhabited, where the intrepid pair often slept out alone beneath the stars, the horse tied to a stake-rope cropping the grass, the rider eating such spare provisions as could be carried in his saddle-bags.

The feat was good, in all the circumstances, but not definitive, for it was carried out on the flat plains, in which the horse was born, with little change of climate, and with good grass and water all the way, and corn occasionally.

How, when or wherefore it came into Tschiffely's head to announce his raid from Buenos Aires to New York is to me as unknown as most of the designs of fate.

Immediately the local Babbitry gave tongue. Old babblers and young bletherers rushed into print to show it was impossible. Just as in Salamanca, when the wise reverend fools proved mathematically and theologically that Columbus was a madman, so did the local wiseacres demonstrate Tschiffely was an ass. No horses, so they said, bred in the plains, almost at sea-level, could cross the Andes, still less endure the Tropics, or bear the constant change of climate and of food upon the road. Indians and bandits would attack the rider; wild beasts destroy the horses; their feet would give out on the stony mountain roads. In fact the project was absurd and would bring ridicule upon the country. Tschiffely took no notice of the arm-chair riders and quietly went on with his few preparations for the start.

They were soon made, and he proceeded to the south, where the most hardy animals are bred, to choose the horses that became national heroes. He selected two, "Mancha," a skewbald, with white legs and face, and streaked all over with white stripes, stocky and with well-made legs and feet, like those of a male mule, as hard as steel. His second choice was "Gato," a yellow dun, for "gato" is a contraction of the word "gateado" (literally, cat-coloured), the favourite colour of the Gauchos of the plains, who always used to choose that colour for hard work. They have a saying, "Gateado, antes muerto que cansado," a dun horse dies before he tires.

Azara, the Spanish naturalist, writing in 1785 (?), says that the great troops of wild horses, known as Baguales, that in his time roamed all over the Pampas, from San Luis to Patagonia, were nearly all either some shade of dun or brown. "Mancha" was fifteen years of age, and "Gato" fourteen, and neither of them had ever eaten corn or worn a shoe.

The horses had just finished a journey of nine hundred miles, taking a troop of cattle from Sarmiento, far below the Welch settlement of Chibut, to Ayacucho in the province of Buenos Aires, in the month of March.

One road and only one was open to him, across the plains to Mendoza, then over the Andes and along the coast of Chile and Peru, from Ecuador to Colombia and through Panama to Nicaragua and on to Mexico.

Once there, Tschiffely knew, all would be easy and the victory assured, for Mexico presented no essential difficulty with its great open plains, and with a population that adored the horse, almost as much as do the Argentines.

Tschiffely set out from Buenos Aires in April, 1925, riding his Mancha and leading Gato with a pack-saddle carrying his food and clothes. Hardly had he started than he encountered torrential rains that turned the "camps" into a morass. He reached Rosario with his horses fresh, finishing his first "étape."

The local know-alls found the horses "extremely weak and thin." This pleased them without doubt, but Dr. Nicholas L. Duro, the veterinary surgeon, saw them with different eyes. After examination he pronounced both horses "in good condition and able to proceed upon their march." In a letter to the local press he said: "It is astonishing that animals of the appearance of these horses, selected for such a journey, and in such disadvantageous conditions, in regard to food, for neither of them has yet learned to eat corn, not only have adapted themselves to the diversity of climate (Rosario is hotter far than Patagonia) but have improved upon the road."

The next eighty leagues were chiefly heavy sand, the water brackish (such water generally purges horses) and the grasses often poisonous, so that the utmost care had to be taken where the horses fed. They crossed the prairies of Santiago del Estero and of Tucuman, and on the twenty-sixth of June arrived at the Bolivian frontier at Perico del Carmen, in the province of Jujuy, having covered twelve hundred miles (400 leagues).

In Tucuman, the curiosity to see the horses and their rider was immense. Somehow or other Mancha's fame as a buck-jumper ("tenia fama de reservado") had preceded him. The officers of the garrison, much against Tschiffely's will, persuaded him to let a soldier, known as a rider, mount the horse. He clapped the spurs into him ("lo buscó"), and then the man, being, in Tschiffely's words, "a dud at the business," after three bucks was thrown into the dirt ("lo basurió"), before the eyes of the whole regiment – not bad work for a grass-fed horse that had just completed more than a thousand miles!

As far as the Bolivian frontier all had been relatively plain sailing for the trio. Although the distance traversed had been great, the horses had been in climates not too widely different from their own. They had not had to swim considerable rivers, and grass and water had been plentiful.

In front of them there lay a Via Crucis.

As they came through the grassy plains, camped underneath the stars by the side of some slow-flowing "arroyo" of the Pampas, Tschiffely, after staking out the horses carefully, would lay down the various pieces of the native saddle ("el recaó"), heat water for his "maté" at a little fire, eat what he had in his saddle-bags and sit smoking, drinking a "maté" or two, and watching the horses eat. When he felt drowsy, he would take a last look at the horses, examine carefully the knot of the stake-rope, look well to the picket-pin, or the bunch of grass if the ground was too hard to drive a pin into, and then lie down with his face in the direction of the way he had to travel at the first streak of dawn.

Leaning upon his elbow he would listen to the mysterious noises of the night, the bark of the Vizcachas, the grunting noise of the burrowing Tuco-tucos, and the shrill neigh of a wild stallion gathering up his mares.

After having taken off his boots, his knife and his revolver ready to his hand, beneath his head, he would draw up his poncho to protect him from the dew. During the night he would rise frequently to make sure the horses were all right. Each time he rose he would look up and mark the constellations as they moved, the Pleiades, Capella and the Southern Cross, with an especial glance at the Tail of Orion, with its three bright stars, the Gauchos used to call "Las Tres Marias." At the false dawn he would awake, shivering and drenched with dew, revive his fire, drink several "matés," and see his horses, half-dozing on their stake-ropes, resting a hind leg, and with their coats dripping and shiny with the dew. Then he would saddle up, taking care not to draw the cinch too tightly if it was Mancha that he was to ride, remembering his fame as a born buckjumper. Putting the pack-saddle on whichever of the horses was to serve that day as cargo bearer ("el carguero"), he would take the halter of the led horse in his right hand, gather up the reins, and mounting lightly, without dwelling for an instant on the stirrup, strike into the jog-trot called in the Argentine "el trotecito," that eats the miles up with less fatigue to rider and horse than any other gait.

The difficulties lay in front. Probably at this point Tschiffely taught his horses to eat corn. He had to face the stony Andean roads, high altitudes, bitter mountain winds, snow, ice, and lack of pasture by the way. All these with horses born in the plains of Patagonia, accustomed to but little variations of temperature and perennial good grass.

Writing from La Quiaca, on the Bolivian frontier, on July 29th (1925), Tschiffely says, "The worst part of the road so far was that between Jujuy and La Quiaca." Sometimes his horses had to pass the night with seventeen and eighteen degrees of frost, without food, in the open tied up to a post, with winds that "penetrated to the bones." He says the horses were improving day by day, only he himself had suffered from a poisoned hand, due to a prick from a sharp thorn. His face, from the exposure to the sun and wind, was like "an English pudding." This reference to our national rice (or perhaps tapioca) "pudding" is scarcely worthy of a horseman of his stamp. In spite of all the prophecies that no horse born on the plain could reach La Quiaca, "Here we are," he says, "the horses fatter than when we set out." His own condition seems to have been so bad that everyone in La Quiaca advised him to give up. "But," he says, "little did they know of the affection that I have to my two 'pingos,' the faithful sharers of so many weary leagues of solitude." "No, sir" (he is writing to Dr. Emilio Solanet, of Buenos Aires, the great horse-breeder), "I will not give up unless either I or my horses die. Good-bye now to the Argentine, regards to all who have accompanied me in their thoughts, with neighs from Mancha and Gato, and their remembrances to all. Yrs. Aimé Tschiffely."

A gallant and tender-hearted letter, that showed a man, brought up in the Swiss mountains, tempered and toughened to the consistency of jerked beef by sun and wind upon the plains, and with a heart of steel.

September saw him in La Paz, the capital of Bolivia, at an altitude of twelve thousand feet. His horses still were in the best of spirits, and he himself had got well of his poisoned hand, in the keen mountain air. The roads had been abominable, snowy at times and always stony and precipitous. From Potosi to Curdo the mountain pass was fifteen thousand feet in height. His guide's mule completely petered out, though mountain-bred, accustomed to high altitudes, and man and mule had to be put aboard the first train, for they were completely "knock-out," as Tschiffely says. His horses plodded on, their rider walking occasionally in the worst bits of the road. During the journey in the mountains he had made generally about two-and-twenty miles a day. A mountain mule seldom makes more, upon an average.

The rider had hurt his leg in a fall on the road, and was suffering from malaria, the horses had been badly bitten by the vampire-bats, but otherwise were well.

La Paz turned out en masse to see the horses and their intrepid rider, and the local veterinary pronounced both Mancha and El Gateado "quite sound in wind and limb." Mancha was so fresh that he nearly kicked his box to pieces when they arrived in Lima and rested for a week or two. In three days they had come from the region of eternal snows into the hottest of the tropics. The trio had been five months on the road, and of the three the rider had suffered most in health. The next stage, between Lima and Trujillo, was more terrible than any of the past.

To read Tschiffely's letter from Barranca (Peru), it seems impossible that even such valiant animals as Mancha and Gato could have survived the hardships of the road. The trail ran through the desert of Mata Caballos ("kill horses"), impossible to pass without a guide. No one was willing to risk his life on such a quest, for he was almost certain to "die in the demand," as goes the Spanish phrase. Full eighteen leagues (54 miles) had to be covered, in a sandy desert, before water could be reached, under a temperature of fifty-two degrees Centigrade, or say a hundred and ten Fahrenheit.

Tschiffely saddled up at half-past four and reached his water at half-past six at night. His description of the "étape" shows him with as light a hand upon the pen as on the reins.

"Sand, sand, and sun, lagoons with myriad of gulls, sand, rocks, and still more sand. Not a plant to be seen, no refuge from the sun that there is fire. To compare the region with the Hell of Dante would be inexact, for nature there is dead; the landscape seems unreal. The horses' feet sank deep into the sand, a burning thirst consumed us. When we arrived at Huecho (where there was a well) the horses, although tired, were going well. My head was like an English 'budin' (this is a variant in spelling, not disagreeable to the eye), my face all the colours of the rainbow, with the skin fit to burst."

There he had to stay a little, for his guide and the mule he rode were quite "knock-out," a favourite phrase of his. As everyone at Huecho knew that the next stage was only possible at night, and to attempt it by day was almost certain failure, there was great difficulty to get a guide willing to undertake the task. Besides the risk of wandering from the right path, or perishing from heat, there was the additional danger, in the next two "étapes" of the dry river-courses swelling to broad torrents impossible to cross, by the sudden melting, up in the Andes, of the snow. This entailed the service of someone who knew the fords, for the unusual heat of the season, extraordinary even in that hell of burning sand, had filled the watercourses a month before the time.

Not finding anyone in Huecho who would affront the perils of the trail, Tschiffely set out on a long tramp of seven leagues, on foot, to a hacienda, where lived a guide who knew the road. He was obliged to go on foot, for on the road there was one of those Andean swinging-rope bridges that no animal could cross. Having found a guide, who in a day or two arrived by a long detour that missed the bridge, riding a mule and leading a horse that carried bread and sardines, with water in four ample flasks. Thirty-two leagues of heavy sand, with neither water nor any food for man or beast, now lay before him. In seventeen hours of "sand and sand and sand" (I quote his letter to *La Nacion* of Buenos Aires, Feb. 16, 1926), almost without a halt, he reached a little Indian village called Huarney. The guide and his two animals were exhausted, but Mancha and El Gateado, when they were unsaddled, rolled in the sand and ate voraciously. Thirty leagues (90 miles) lay between Huarney and Casura, another Indian town. When he arrived at the Casura river it was in high flood, and he was forced to swim. Riding his Gateado and leading Mancha, he plunged into the stream. Swept down the current he was almost drowned with both his horses. The cowardly guide, who after much persuasion tried the ford, did nothing to assist him and almost by a miracle they all reached the bank. That day they travelled twenty hours, with only one hour's rest, after the passage of the ford. His horses, as he wrote (to *La Nacion*), though tired, were not exhausted, but the guide and his horses were nearly dead. The sandy deserts now were passed, but perils of a different nature still lay before him on the road.

One more he was obliged to plunge into the Andes, for no road ran along the coast to Panama. So he set off for Quito, having already passed by Cuzco, the other Inca capital, on his Andean journey from Bolivia to Peru. By this time notices of the "Raid" began to appear in every city of the Americas. The sporting circles of New York and Mexico received reports of Tschiffely's journey from every wireless station on the way. "Mancha" and "Gato" had become household words in every newspaper.

All unknown to himself, Tschiffely was entering on the most arduous and dangerous portion of his ride. The frost and snows of the high Andes, the burning heat of the coastal sands between Lima and Trujillo, the poisonous pasturage in Jujuy, were all as nothing to what he soon was called on to endure. At least in all the countries he had passed through there had been food for man and beast. Scanty at times, but still sufficient to sustain their strength; water, except between Lima and Trujillo, had never failed, and there had been no danger from wild beasts. Once he left Quito, at an altitude of ten thousand feet, straight from the coast, over the roughest mountain roads, he woud be obliged to plunge into the forests of some of the hottest tropics of the world. Those forests swarming with vampire-bats, with every kind of noxious insect, full of dangerous snakes, cut by deep streams, the haunt of alligators and electric eels, with every shallow the abode of stinging rays, that if a horse treads on them, inflict a wound that causes agony and does not heal for months; peopled by shoals of the voracious little fish, the Piranha, that tears to pieces every living thing that has the smallest open wound upon it, constituted an obstacle difficult and dangerous beyond belief. Their recesses sheltered tigers (jaguars) powerful enough to kill a horse with a blow of their paw and drag his body fifty or a hundred yards. Moreover, little grass grows under the dark trees, and in the rare clearings such pasture as there is, is wiry, hard, and carries little nourishment. The leaves of a certain palm tree, called pindó, are eaten by the native animals, but it was quite uncertain whether horses accustomed to the sweet grasses of the Patagonian plains would eat them or, having eaten, thrive upon them.

To reach Quito from Piura, on the coast, an arduous journey lay in front of him, of about three hundred miles. If in Peru and Bolivia the intrepid trio had been objects of interest to all, in Ecuador the enthusiasm reached its height. At the first frontier town the authorities and all the "notables," civil and military alike, turned out to greet "Los fenómenos de las Pampas Argentinas." The country people rivalled the authorities in the warmness of their welcome, and their curiosity.

Mancha and Gato, once the frontier of Ecuador was passed, seem to have been almost deified. Deification, even if spontaneous by the adorers, and involuntary on the part of the subjects, has its inconveniences. Tschiffely, with the "pawky" humour that distinguishes both Scots and Swiss alike, writes in a letter to *La Nacion* that the attention with which his horses and himself were treated made him lose much time, when he had rather have been resting, in answering questions at every place at which they stopped. He had to tell his adventures to all and sundry for a hundred times.

In fact, his progress, through such parts of Ecuador as were inhabited, reminds one of a parliamentary candidate on an election tour, dragged to and fro by his supporters, always obliged to smile and to repeat the self-same "boniment." Even the horses suffered, for the people gathered round to see them feed, and gaze at them with that fixed and apparently uncomprehending stare natural to the Indians of Ecuador and Bolivia.

The road as far as Alausi, some fifty leagues short of the capital, was only to be described as devilish.

It ran beside the railway line from Guayaquil to Quito and was a series of ups and downs after the fashion of a switchback. The heat was terrible, the tracks a "razorback" bordered on each side by a sea of mud. At night the temperature fell below freezing-point, and the rain was perpetual.

The troops of mules that, since the Conquest, had plied upon the road carrying all merchandise from the coast to Quito, had made a sort of staircase of the track, leaving great steps, called "camellones" locally. Sometimes the descents were so precipitous and slippery in the deep mud that Mancha and Gato slid down them seated on their haunches, with their forefeet stretched out in front of them. This feat the mules born in the country all understand and practise and many of the older books of travel have woodcuts showing them at work.

To Mancha and Gato this was new, but it was wonderful that they at once learned to execute the feat as to the manner born. The wretched halting-places, called by the ancient "Inca term of tambos," were filthy in the extreme, malodorous and full of every flying and crawling insect that made life miserable.

Mules and their drivers, pigs, dogs, asses and chickens, slept promiscuously in the corrals attached to the "tambos." Great care had to be exercised that the horses' forage was not stolen or that they were not kicked by any of the mules. All these inconveniences and the state of the road spun out the journey between the coast and Quito for two months.

The horses reached Quito perfectly well and pulling at their bits, but Tschiffely had suffered greatly in his health from hardships and malaria, bad water and execrable food. He had to stop in Quito for six weeks, most of the time in hospital.

The horses, in a hacienda of a Colonel Sturdy, fed on the best of pasture, and waxed fat, getting into such good condition that when Tschiffely, his health restored, mounted them to give an exhibition of their quality, at the request of the authorities of Quito, they jumped about like colts. Gato went at everything with a rush, passing through mudholes in a plunge or two and crossing rotten bridges without looking at them. Mancha, upon the contrary, if he had to pass a doubtful bridge, tried it with his near front foot, looked at it carefully and only ventured on it after putting down his head to bring his ears and eyes and nostrils on a level with the planks. ("Quel destrier, aveva l'ingegno á maraviglia.")

The first part of the journey to the Colombian frontier, although an eight months' drought had dried up all the pastures, was relatively easy, for there actually were roads.

Through the hot valleys between Pasto and Popayan, unhealthy, mostly composed of forest, where no doubt tigers abounded, and if they camped Tschiffely must have been obliged to light a fire and watch his horses all the night, ready to stand by their heads and quiet them if a tiger's cry were wafted ominously through the woods. From Pasto the route lay through Cali and down the Cauca valley to Medellin, the capital of the State of Antioquia.

All three of the adventurers suffered terribly upon the way. Alternately, sometimes on the same day, they had to climb up into the Andes and endure cold, snow and icy winds, and then descend into the steamy valleys, where the damp heat rendered it hard to breathe, and the perpetual rain rotted the rider's clothes. Writing from Bogotá on the the 10th of October, 1926, after eighteen months upon the road, Tschiffely gives an account of all that they endured. He reveals also his undaunted spirit and his sympathetic attitude to the companions of his extraordinary feat.

Eight months of drought, he says, had burned up everything, "and my poor horses used to stand at the pasture gate, waiting for me at sunrise, without having eaten anything. It would be difficult to express what I felt on such occasions, especially when I was saddling up at sunrise. The poor animals looked at me with the eyes of children, and Mancha, always a 'talker' ('charlatán'), neighed, as it were asking me for what I could not give him, perhaps for ten or twelve hours," after an arduous day.

When Medellin was reached Tschiffely received confirmation of what he had already heard in Lima as to the impossibility of travelling by land to Panama.

The Government of Colombia, through the Argentine Legation at Bogotá, sent to inform Tschiffely that the journey was impossible. No roads existed through the virgin forests that had never yet been trodden by the foot of man. Swamps, lakes and rivers, without bridges, swarming with alligators and with banks so swampy that it would prove impossible, even after crossing, ever to emerge upon hard ground alive, set up a barrier impossible to cross. The forests were quite uninhabited, even by wild Indians. In fact few portions of the globe are more inhospitable or more unknown; few more unhealthy.

Tschiffely went by train and mule-back to Bogotá, only to receive the same report from the Colombian Government. Nothing remained but to embark the horses as far as Panama, but before doing so he obtained a statement from the authorities of the district of the Choco that borders on the Gulf of Darien. In it they said that from personal knowledge of the country any journey from their district into Panama must of necessity result in the death both of the rider and the horses. They alleged once more the lack of roads, the denseness of the virgin woods and the fact that they had remained as unknown as at the creation of the world.

During his journey by mule-back to Bogotá, he left his horses in a fenced pasture ("potrero") where there was abundant grass. A river ran through it, and an Indian boy gave them two baths a day, and twice a day they fed on sugar-cane, unrefined sugar ("panela"), bran, and a grass called "pasto imperial" that has great nutritive power.

Forced to perform the journey from Medellin to Panama in a river steamboat, a mere step in comparison with the fifteen thousand miles from Buenos Aires to New York, he arrived safely at the Canal, and after fifteen days of quarantine was one more ready for the road.

His spirits rose, his horses were in good condition after their long rest, and he knew the country that lay ahead of him would prove but child's play after that he had just passed. Writing to *La Nacion*, he says: "Once I have passed the State of Costa Rica, where I am told there are bits of the road that present difficulties, the rest is easy.

"I hope in eight, or perhaps nine months to be safely in New York.

"For my part I assure you all that I can do, I shall do. I have no fear of the results and I shall never give up, if it is possible to go forward, and the same supplies to both the horses ('pingos'), I feel sure."

The trio crossed the Canal on a drawbridge, not that they would have been afraid to swim it, for Tschiffely says, " 'We' have swum rivers far wider than the Canal."

Just after crossing the Canal, the first accident occurred, for up till then neither of the horses had hurt itself, or suffered anything particular except cold, hunger, heat and the attacks of vampire-bats.

Riding along a muddy trail, Mancha stepped on a piece of half buried rusty wire and cut his foreleg deeply, but, luckily, not near the tendons. The wound was deep and cost them three weeks of delay till it was healed and Mancha ready for the road.

Although he had been told that difficulties awaited him upon the road to San Jośe de Costa Rica, Tschiffely had no idea that they would be so great. The trail from Panama to the little mountain town of David ran through the forests and was deep in mud. Although he took two guides, they lost the track, and wandered helplessly in the vast jungles, all bound together with lianas, into an almost impenetrable mass.

To regain the lost trail, they were obliged to open what is known as a "picada" with the "machetes" (bush knives) that in those countries every horseman carries at his saddle bow.

Food for the horses there was none except the leaves of a scrub oak and a dwarf palm-tree.

The horses' shoes came off in the thick mud. Tschiffely says with pride, "However, they could travel well enough without them." The rain never ceased for an instant, so that his clothes all became rotten, even his boots rotted off from his feet, and he was obliged to tie the soles on to his feet with strips of hide, for, unlike the horses, he could not travel without shoes.

Malaria once more attacked him, and all he had to fight it off with was the native rum, fiery and raw that, when you swallow it, goes like a torchlight procession down the throat.

When he arrived at San José de Costa Rica in a torrential rain after a forced march of eight leagues, a deputation waited on him with an invitation to a banquet. He was wet to the skin, his boots were sandals tied to his feet with strips of hide. After he had seen Mancha and Gato led off in honour, guests of the Legation of the Argentine, his head whirling with the champagne that he was forced to drink, he staggered to his room in the hotel. A bed with sheets, the first he had seen for months, was so inviting that, wet through as he was, without attempting even to remove his fragmentary boots, he threw himself upon it, and fell asleep. He says he was exhausted, but that the horses were as fresh as when they had started out from Panama.

His health obliged him to remain for several weeks in Panama. As Nicaragua was in a state bordering on anarchy, a prey to the contending factions, swarming with bandits and disbanded soldiers, and horses were extremely scarce, and, of course, contraband of war, he was obliged once more to embark his horses a little distance from Puntarenas (Costa Rica) to La Union in Salvador.

The journey through that small republic was not difficult, but the heat was so intense that it brought out a new attack of the malaria, and in San Salvador (the capital of the republic of El Salvador) he was laid up another fifteen days. His strength exhausted by the hardships of the road and the attacks of fever that he suffered from, he doubted for the first time since he left Buenos Aires of his ultimate success.

However, when he reached Guatemala City, at an altitude of six thousand feet, he soon revived in spirits and in health.

"We" were warmly welcomed by the inhabitants and the Government; society and the learned institutions all joined in honouring "us." The phrase shows the man's character, as well as a whole volume of his "life and miracles." Mancha and Gato, without doubt, were flattered by the attention of the "cultured institutions," and if they could have spoken would probably have done as well as or better than many orators such institutions endure and suffer under.

Tschiffely now felt certain of success. Mexico was a land where gentlemen and horsemen ("caballero") were synonymous. The country on the whole was not so difficult as any through which he had already passed. His hopes ran high, and in a week or two he thought he would be in the capital (Mexico).

But as the Spanish proverb has it, a hare springs up when you are not expecting her. ("Adonde menos se piensa, salta la lie bre.")

Not far from the bridge at the frontier Gato went lame for the first time since leaving Buenos Aires. At Tapachula he could go no farther. Luckily there was a military post of cavalry. The veterinary surgeon found that the smith in Guatemala had driven a nail into the foot. He cut it out at once, but the hot climate and the perpetual moisture of the rainy season inflamed the wound so much that Tschiffely passed three or four nights, so to speak, at the bedside of the sufferer, applying fomentations to the foot. Gato was almost well, when some "son of a mother who never yet said No" let loose overnight a strange horse in the stable-yard. Next morning Gato had received so terrible a kick on his near foreleg that he could not lie down. The leg swelled up enormously and everyone told Tschiffely that the best thing that he could do was to shoot Gato and end his misery.

"It was a rude blow and I was overwhelmed with grief, but I would not even entertain the idea of losing the good horse, companion of 'our' perils on the road."

At once he telegraphed to the Argentine Ambassador in the capital,

Señor Roberto Labougli, who replied asking him to send the horse by train to Mexico, where he would be cared for by the best veterinaries.

These delays made him lose a month, but nothing daunted, having procured a guide and bought two horses for him, he once more started out upon the road.

Three or four days' journey convinced him that he would never reach the capital alone, for the road swarmed with bandits and with revolutionaries, words that, as he says, in Mexico have the same meaning.

At the next military post the Commandant refused to let him pass, saying he could not respond for his security if he went an alone.

Hearing the case, the President of the Republic, General Elias Calles, sent out a troop of cavalry to escort Tschiffely on the road.

This was a "gesture," as he says, of "the greatest generosity and sympathy to the Argentine Republic never before accorded to a mere traveller." The truth was that Mexico was all agog to see the "heroes" of the raid.

At every town and hamlet that he passed the inhabitants turned out to greet him, patting and making much of Mancha and doing all that lay within their power to help them on their way.

Even in the humble ranchos of the Indians "they did their best to succour and assist us."

The rains delayed the journey, and the cavalry were not well mounted, so that when they reached Oscara, Mancha alone was not exhausted.

The rivers, too, were swollen with the rains and, as there were no bridges, had to be crossed swimming – a dangerous operation, as they swarmed with alligators. As he advanced amidst general rejoicing, encountering a cooler climate day by day, for the interior plateau of the country ("la meseta de Anahuac") stands at an elevation of six thousand feet, the road grew easier.

At Puebla, the people had arranged a festival "to welcome us," but as fate willed it, he had at once to take to bed, for several days prostrated by malaria.

When he reached Mexico his entry was a triumph, and was telegraphed at once to the whole world.

The streets were packed and as he rode along on Mancha, women came out upon the balconies and showered flowers upon him.

"My joy was without limit, and my feelings unforgettable, when I saw 'friend Gato' ('el amigo Gato') led up quite fresh, and as sound as when he was a colt," owing to the care he had received from the State veterinary, Señor Labougle. During his sojourn in the city he received enormous hospitality from all classes of society, the President himself visiting the horses several times and admiring them.

On the 27th of November he set his face towards the frontier of the United States, leaving a host of friends in Mexico, with both his horses fresh and bounding under him. All through Mexico Tschiffely's journey was a triumphal march, for the news of his coming had been telegraphed from Mexico to every town upon the way. His stages were erratic, for at times more than a hundred horsemen turned out to escort him on his way. The smallest hamlet hoisted the Argentine flag, sometimes made out of coloured paper, and the nine hundred miles to New Laredo, the frontier town upon the Rio Grande, was like a street during a carnival, that is to say, when they passed through a town. I, who have ridden the whole distance from San Antonio, Texas, to Mexico, and back again, when all the road was perilous from the attacks of the apaches near the frontier, and of the bandits, nearer Mexico, though I remember every village he passed through, can hardly take in the changed circumstances. Across the frontier the authorities had organized a military pageant in honour "of the brave horseman of the Argentine and his two faithful friends." Tschiffely, mounted on Mancha and holding Gato by his side, took the salute, as the troops with their bands playing passed before him. It must have been the proudest moment of his life, and have repaid him for all that he had undergone on his fantastic journey of fifteen thousand miles.

Two thousand kilometres still lay between the frontier and his goal, and perils of a sort he had looked for still awaited him. He had hoped to reach New York in June, but invitations, banquets and interviews rained on him. If he had not protested, escorts of cavalry would have accompanied him all through Texas. In San Antonio he was obliged to stay for fifteen days, the guest of the municipality. The same thing happened in Austin, Houston, Fort Worth and Dallas, and invitations from towns far off his route flowed in upon him. When in Fort Worth a compatriot, Don Gustavo Muñiz Barreto, fitted him out with a complete Gaucho costume, "poncho," and wide Turkish trousers, tucked into high patent-leather boots, with silver trappings for his horse. Public enthusiasm knew no bounds.

Mancha, on account of his striking colour, was the idol of "las bellas Yanquis," who flocked to see him every day, patting and petting him. They grew so demonstrative in their affection that Tschiffely had to keep strict guard over Mancha or they would have cut off all his mane and tail to keep as souvenirs.

Mancha, who, as we know, enjoyed "fame as a buckjumper" ("tenia fama de reservado") became so irritable that it was dangerous to go near him; but Gato, more apathetic, took everything "con apatia," and was concerned entirely with the good things of the stable, which he consumed with great enthusiasm.

Both of them grew as fat as Jeshurun, but there is no recorded instance of their ever having kicked.

Once more the local wiseacres shook their long ears and solemnly announced that no horse in the world could stand more than a day or two upon the treated roads. In spite of that, Mancha and Gato advanced steadily, doing their thirty miles a day, passing by St. Louis, Missouri, Indianapolis, and Washington.

As they drew nearer to New York the danger that they ran from the continuous stream of automobiles on the roads was as great as on any portion of his adventurous road. As he rode on, in constant peril from the motor traffic, his mind dwelt always on his goal, and on the joy that he would feel when once again he and his horses arrived safely in Buenos Aires, where, after all their perils and hard work, Gato and Mancha could forget for ever girths, bits and saddles, and the hardships of the road. His dream is fulfilled, and the two faithful companions of his wanderings once more are back again in their own country, after having travelled fifteen thousand miles during their three years' raid. Happier than mankind, they have their Trapalanda upon earth, eat the sweet grasses of their native plains, drink the soft, muddy water of some "arroyo," and though they know it not, never again "the cruel spur shall make them weary."